# LOYALTY

## THE REACH OF THE NOBLE HEART

# BOB SORGE

OASIS HOUSE
LEE'S SUMMIT, MISSOURI, USA

*Other books by Bob Sorge:*

- *UNRELENTING PRAYER (2005 release)*
- *FOLLOWING THE RIVER: A Vision For Corporate Worship*
- *ENVY: The Enemy Within*
- *SECRETS OF THE SECRET PLACE*
- *Secrets Of The Secret Place COMPANION STUDY GUIDE*
- *GLORY: When Heaven Invades Earth*
- *DEALING WITH THE REJECTION AND PRAISE OF MAN*
- *PAIN, PERPLEXITY, AND PROMOTION: A prophetic interpretation of the book of Job*
- *THE FIRE OF GOD'S LOVE*
- *THE FIRE OF DELAYED ANSWERS*
- *IN HIS FACE: A prophetic call to renewed focus*
- *EXPLORING WORSHIP: A practical guide to praise and worship*
- *Exploring Worship WORKBOOK & DISCUSSION GUIDE*

LOYALTY: THE REACH OF THE NOBLE HEART
Copyright © 2004 by Bob Sorge
Published by Oasis House
P.O. Box 127
Greenwood, Missouri 64034-0127
www.oasishouse.net

All Scripture quotations are from the New King James Version of the Bible. Copyright © 1979, 1980, 1982, Thomas Nelson Inc., Publisher. Used by permission.

Edited by Edie Veach. Cover design by Kevin Keller.

Printed in the United States of America

International Standard Book Number: 0-9704791-7-4

Library of Congress Cataloging-in-Publication Data

Sorge, Bob.
    Loyalty : the reach of the noble heart / Bob Sorge.
       p. cm.
    Includes bibliographical references.
    ISBN 0-9704791-7-4 (pbk.)
    1. Loyalty--Religious aspects--Christianity. 2. Loyalty--Biblical teaching. 1.Title

    BV4647.L6S67 2004
    24'.4--dc22

2004041567

# *What Others Are Saying*

While we can celebrate healings and miracles, the real core of building strong local churches that transform society requires the recovery of loyalty. I am personally convinced that loyalty is a core value that cannot be side-stepped, ignored, or discarded if we intend to see a genuine release of apostolic authority in the earth and the greatest ingathering the church or the world has ever witnessed. I know from first-hand experience that there will be a Korah who rises up against us, an Absalom we have raised that deeply wounds us, a Judas who betrays us, and even a Peter who denies us. Oh yes, there will also be a Pilate to crucify us at some juncture. Our ability to embrace these moments as opportunities for growth is priceless.

Bob takes us on a spiritual pilgrimage and invites us to examine both the promises of loving loyalty and the dangers of violating it. His keen prophetic insights on Lucifer's rebellion and the response of the Father in eternity past are of themselves worth the read of the entire book. The message of this book is timeless in its value, and relevant to the times we live in. You can't afford to ignore what this prophetic teacher in the Body of Christ has to say within these pages. May this treatise find wide exposure amongst both leaders and followers and may it bear fruit that will be evidenced in the outworking of our covenant relationship with God and each other.

Mark J. Chironna, PhD
Pastor, The Master's Touch International Church
Orlando, Florida

Disloyalty in the church does more damage to the work of God than all the demons of hell. Still, we don't hear much about it. In his book, Loyalty: The Reach Of The Noble Heart, Bob Sorge faces this problem head on in a loving exposition of the life of David. All Christians should read it carefully and Christian leaders need to examine it prayerfully. Loyalty is both fundamental and foundational. Without it, there is little hope of continuity and perpetuation of what God is doing in His church. This book should be required reading before a person is ordained to Christian service.

Judson Cornwall
Author and Teacher
Phoenix, Arizona


Presently, two facts confront thinking believers: (1) we live in earth's final era, and (2) the "worthy" and "noble" are decreasingly valued. If there is one virtue that can bring and sustain substance to and relevance through our lives—the "stuff" that always makes the difference for good and for God in the world—it's loyalty. Bob Sorge has mined this concept and its truth for us, and placed a wealth of its "worthy" before us. I pray a whole generation of Christians might be shaped by the substance-filled life-and-power values fostered through this book.

Jack W. Hayford
Pastor, The Church On The Way
Chancellor, The King's Seminary
Van Nuys, California


Wow! What a book! What a message! What conviction! "Loyalty: The Reach Of The Nobel Heart," is a singularly important and timely message for every leader and servant of God. From the secret place in God's presence, Bob brings one of the most powerful and liberating truths I have ever read.

This message of "What is Biblical Loyalty and Disloyalty" is almost a non-existent issue in the body of Christ. When was the last time you heard or read anything about Biblical Loyalty? As a result, many leaders in the body of Christ have been crippled by betrayal and disloyalty. And because of this crippling disease in the leadership, the body is also crippled. But the good news is, healing is on the way. This book will challenge you to step beyond the pain of betrayal toward a course of healing and spiritual transformation. Are you ready to begin a life-changing journey? Get reading because healing is on the way!

Sam Hinn
Pastor, The Gathering Place Worship Center
Lake Mary, Florida


Living in the last days, as we are, we are warned that there will be "truce-breakers"—the opposite of loyalty. Bob Sorge has caught hold of the spirit of loyalty, which operates out of love. This book should be a manual in churches and fellowships to encourage true spiritual unity by loyalty to a Person.

Paul Johansson
President, Elim Bible Institute
Lima, New York


Bob Sorge's book "Loyalty: The Noble Reach of the Heart" provokes me because Bob is a friend who provokes me. I am provoked because Bob lives what he says, practices what he writes. He is loyal to weaker friends because he knows the kindness of God in his own place of weakness. He is loyal to friends of greater influence because he is settled in what God has given him for this season of his life. He is loyal to the Lord, knowing that Jesus is his only hope for strength and courage in a time of waiting for deliverance. You will want to read this book, for the man and the message are the same, and it is a privilege to be instructed by one such as he.

Gary Wiens
Burning Heart Ministries & the International House of Prayer
Kansas City, Missouri

# *Dedication*

## TO SYLVIA EVANS

When I think of my friends who demonstrate a loyal spirit, none is more deserving of honor than you, Sylvia. You are loyal to your friends, to your spiritual overseers, to your confidantes, to your parents and family, to your coworkers and colleagues in ministry, and most of all, to your Lord. Your example adds credibility to the weight of your message. You are a role model and spiritual mother to many. The Lord's grace has made of you a vessel that can be safely entrusted with spiritual authority. Your children are loyal to you.

# *Acknowledgements*

Writing this book was a team effort. The front cover photo concept was Tim Spirk's idea—thanks, Tim! And on the book content I had a small army of friends who gave me very helpful feedback. My sincere thanks to my wife, Marci; my parents, Arvin & Irma Sorge; my brother, Sheldon, and his wife, Tammy; David Oaks; Lee Simmons; Paul Johannson; David Edwards; Jeff Ell; Jeff James; Mike Bickle; Ed Chinn; Pat Prior; Sylvia Evans; Sue Curran; and Phil Stern. Your input was invaluable!

Thanks, Edie, for your editorial help, and Kevin, for the cover design.

Above all, thank You, Lord Jesus, for Your loyalty to us!

# Contents

# INTRODUCTION

**W**hen was the last time you read a book on loyalty? There aren't many out there. Why is the topic seemingly avoided? It may be because those who are most qualified to speak on it could appear self-serving if they did so.

It's more than coincidental that the Lord has prompted me to write this book at a time when I do not pastor a church or lead any kind of ministry team. My motive in writing this book, therefore, is simply to serve other ministry teams in the body of Christ and to extol the magnificence of this wondrous virtue.

This book is not primarily a warning about the distress you could experience if you give your heart in loyalty to the wrong person. Clearly, we need discernment in whom to be loyal to, and I will endeavor to warn about the inherent dangers. However, the primary thrust of this book will be positive. *Our fundamental premise is that loyalty is a precious pearl that deserves to be intentionally pursued and cultivated.*

It may be one of the most misunderstood biblical principles in the church today, so we have many important questions to explore, such as: What is loyalty, and why should we value it? How can we know when it's safe to give our heart to a leader? How can a leader prove himself worthy of being followed? How can we guard against disloyalty?

This book is a call to biblical loyalty—first to God and then to God's Davids. God's Davids are those leaders—male or female—who, like David of old, have a pure heart to seek the face of Jesus Christ and His Kingdom without regard to personal fame or inurement. They share David's "one thing" passion of Psalm 27:4, "One thing I have desired of the LORD, that will I seek: That I may dwell in the house of the LORD all the days of my life, to behold the beauty of the LORD, and to inquire in His temple." Since they don't have a self-serving or ambitious agenda, they shepherd the flock of God in faithfulness.

### User-Friendly Tips

David has been established in Scripture as the foremost example (beyond Christ Himself) of a true servant leader to whom God is loyal and toward whom God expects others to be loyal. And, because of the detail given to his story, David's son, Absalom, is the foremost biblical example of disloyalty (with Judas Iscariot running a close second). I will make repeated references, therefore, to the David/Absalom story. If it's been a while since you've read the story about Absalom, I recommend that you read the Appendix now, which is a brief summary of Absalom's treachery. Refresh yourself on that story so this book will have maximum meaning for you.

My mention of "fathers" in this book is not intended to be gender-specific; I am merely using the language of Malachi 4:6 which speaks of God's turning the hearts of fathers to their children. The principles of this book are relevant, therefore, to both mothers and fathers, as well as to sons and daughters.

Use this book as a springboard for dialogue in your leadership team. The discussion questions in each chapter are designed to help your team hear each others' hearts. The purpose of this book is to promote unity among ministry team members and business teams. My prayer is that team members will gain a passion to be loyal to God's David on their team, and that God's leaders will be inspired to be Davidic leaders to whom it is safe to be loyal. As you approach this subject prayerfully, may the Holy Spirit enlighten the eyes of your understanding to the power of this glorious virtue and its implications for your team's future together.

# PART ONE
## *Loyalty To God*

Our discussion must start with God—the Originator and Fountain-head of all things. God is loyal, so loyalty is of God. His loyal heart is the thing that empowers us to be loyal to Him.

# CHAPTER 1

# *God's Search For Loyalty*

**W**hen God scrolls across the landscape of humanity, there is one character quality above all others that He is specifically looking for:

For the eyes of the LORD run to and fro throughout the whole earth, to show Himself strong on behalf of those whose heart is loyal to Him (2 Chronicles 16:9).

This verse describes an intense, high-speed search. *The hunt is on, and the object of God's search is loyalty.* In God's value system, loyalty is esteemed as a commodity of great worth.[1] It is so valuable to God that, according to this Scripture, God will reveal the power of His right hand to those who possess it.

God told Ezekiel, "'So I sought for a man'" (Ezekiel 22:30). God is always searching, and the object of His search is for a loyal man or woman. Once He finds a Noah, He can send a flood. Once He finds a Joseph, He can give Pharaoh a divine dream. Once He has an Elijah, He can turn a nation around. When He has a Jesus of Nazareth, He can save the world. God is always looking for loyalty because, once he finds a loyal heart, He can do mighty things in the earth.

God wants a huge family whose hearts are all turned to Him in adoring loyalty. God is in the business of "bringing many sons to glory" (Hebrews 2:10). He wants many sons who are just like Jesus—truly loyal even unto death. And He's chosen you to be part of that family!

*God is looking for loyalty—because it's a God-quality.* It is a divine

---

[1] See 1 Chronicles 28:9; 1 Kings 8:61.

attribute that pulsates at the core of the everlasting Trinity, defining the very personality of God. No one is loyal like God.

### Loyalty Within The Trinity

The Father is radically loyal to the Son. On two occasions He literally thundered from the skies, "'This is My beloved Son, in whom I am well pleased.'"[2] God was loyal to Moses and the prophets, but now His only begotten Son was living on the earth, and the Father wanted to establish beyond all doubt that His loyalty to the Son surpassed any other.

The Father is determined that all of creation will bow down and worship before His Son. The name of the Son will be exalted above every other name.[3] The Son has not yet been vindicated. His name is still cursed and reproached every day by sinners. But all that is going to change. Just wait and see—the day is coming when the Son's reputation will be exonerated and He will be extolled more than any other. The Father's loyalty will guarantee it.

The Father is *so* loyal to the Son that, if anyone tries to approach Him via a different route, God refuses to be found. "'Nor is there salvation in any other, for there is no other name under heaven given among men by which we must be saved'" (Acts 4:12).

A seeker might ask, "But why can we not find salvation through Mohammed or Confucius or some other good man?" The answer has to do with God's loyalty. He is singularly loyal to the Son whom He sent into the world and is absolutely not to any other would-be savior. *The Father is so loyal to His only begotten Son that He is greatly offended when people dismiss the Person of His appointed King.*

The Son is equally loyal to the Father, something Jesus demonstrated when He said, "'I always do those things that please Him.'"[4] Everything Jesus did on earth was an expression of His loyalty to God, for He desired the Father to be glorified through everything He did.[5] *The ultimate demonstration of the Son's loyalty was when He died on the cross—all to fulfill the Father's plan.*

The Holy Spirit is also deeply loyal, something Jesus was referring

[2] Matthew 3:17; 17:5.
[3] Philippians 2:9-11.
[4] John 8:29.

to when He said of the Holy Spirit, "'He will glorify Me, for He will take of what is Mine and declare it to you'" (John 16:14). Jesus had absolutely no misgivings about passing His ministry b*aton to the Holy Spirit because He knew of the Spirit's undying loyalty.* Every time we preach the greatness of Jesus, we can know that the Holy Spirit will be present, without fail, to confirm the message with convicting power.

*The fidelity of the Father, Son, and Holy Spirit—One God, three Persons—is our template for true loyalty.*

### *Seeking To Be Like God*

The Scriptures implore us, "Pursue...godliness."[6] Godliness is simply the quality of being like God. Since God is loyal, the godly will reach for loyalty.

A loyal spirit is a godly quality that is both pursued and given. We strive for it, and yet recognize it comes from God. David acknowledged that when he prayed, "'And give my son Solomon a loyal heart to keep Your commandments and Your testimonies and Your statutes.'"[7] Loyalty is given to the heart from the Spirit of God.

God empowers us with a loyal spirit so that we might be loyal, first of all, to Him. *Loyalty to God is our first and greatest mandate.* David said, "'As for you, my son Solomon, know the God of your father, and serve Him with a loyal heart.'"[8] Solomon in turn said to the people, "'Let your heart therefore be loyal to the LORD our God, to walk in His statutes and keep His commandments.'"[9]

The New Testament puts it in these terms: "Let us draw near with *a true heart* in full assurance of faith."[10] "A true heart" is a heart that is loyal to God without any shadow of duplicity or hypocrisy.

If we should be placed in circumstances where we must choose to be loyal either to man or God, there is no question what our decision would be. "But Peter and the other apostles answered and said: 'We ought to obey God rather than men'" (Acts 5:29). God always comes

---

[5] See John 17:4.
[6] 1 Timothy 6:11; see also 1 Timothy 4:7.
[7] 1 Chronicles 29:19.
[8] 1 Chronicles 28:9.
[9] 1 Kings 8:61.

first. Our loyalty to God is to supercede even our loyalty to our own family members.[11]

### Dove's Eyes

What does it mean to be loyal to God? It means three things to me. First, it means to give Him my unwavering love and to never share my affections with another. I am espoused to Him,[12] which means we have come into a relationship of exclusive intimacy.

The Lord says that we have "dove's eyes."[13] This truth became more meaningful to me after a certain regrettable event. I was driving down the highway one day at about 50 miles per hour, and in the distance I could see a pair of turtledoves slowly waddling out onto the highway. As I approached them I thought to myself, "You better move. I don't swerve for birds or animals." (I've heard of enough car accidents where the driver swerved to avoid an animal or bird and hit a person instead.) But they just kept on meandering out onto the road. By the time they saw me, it was too late. BAM! I hit them both at 50 m.p.h. Looking in my rearview mirror, I saw a plume of feathers billowing into the air behind me. As I drove away I thought to myself, "Stupid birds. Should have moved."

It was later that I learned: *Turtledoves have no peripheral vision.* The lovebirds didn't even see me coming!

When Jesus tells us we have dove's eyes, He is saying, "You have eyes for Me only. I am all that you can see. Your head is not turned to other loves. I am your only desire." Jesus' affirmation only strengthens my resolve. I will behold Him only and will not allow my eyes to turn after any other affection. For me, this is loyalty.

*His heart burns for but one Bride; my heart yearns to reciprocate with like passions of exclusive devotion.* My weak heart may not match the perfection of His loyalty, but I'm reaching for it!

### Loyalty: Looking To God Alone

So, the first thing loyalty means to me is that I reserve my heart af-

---

[10] Hebrews 10:22, emphasis added.
[11] See Deuteronomy 13:6-9.
[12] 2 Corinthians 11:2.
[13] Song of Solomon 1:15; 4:1.

fections for Him only. Second, it means that I look to Him alone as the source of my salvation and deliverance and help.

God wants to be my only Source. This truth is at the heart of our primary text for this book:

> For the eyes of the LORD run to and fro throughout the whole earth, to show Himself strong on behalf of those whose heart is loyal[14] to Him (2 Chronicles 16:9).

Let's look at the story behind this verse. When Asa, king of Jerusalem in the southern kingdom of Judah, was young and newly installed as king, a million-man army from Ethiopia rose up against him and invaded the land.[15] Asa was inexperienced in warfare and trembled in fear before this mighty force. So he cried out to the Lord for help. In response, God intervened and sovereignly struck the Ethiopian army, giving Asa the victory. Now, Asa had his own personal history with God. He had seen God perform the impossible on his behalf and deliver him.

Move the clock forward thirty-six years. Asa was now a veteran, experienced in running his kingdom and in doing battle. God had blessed him, so his kingdom was significantly stronger than when he assumed the throne. He had accrued wealth, armies, and war equipment. Once again Asa's kingdom came under attack, but this time the invading king was Baasha, king of Samaria (Israel's northern kingdom).[16] What would Asa do this time? Would he call on God again, since he had known the delivering power of God? Or would he rely on the resources he had accumulated over thirty-six years?

Unfortunately, Asa made an unwise decision. He hired the king of Syria to attack Baasha. It seemed like a logical enough plan since he now had the wealth to buy the Syrian's help. And on the surface Asa's strategy worked. Syria accepted the money and attacked Baasha's forces, causing Baasha to withdraw from Judah. But even though Asa achieved the desired end, the way he accomplished it did not please the Lord.

---

[13] Song of Solomon 1:15; 4:1.

[14] The original Hebrew word that the NKJV translates as "loyal"—shalem— means to be perfect, complete, sound, in a state of wholeness and unity.

[15] See 2 Chronicles 14.

So the Lord sent Hanani to Asa with the words we have quoted above, "'For the eyes of the LORD run to and fro throughout the whole earth, to show Himself strong on behalf of those whose heart is loyal to Him. In this you have done foolishly; therefore from now on you shall have wars.'" Hanani was basically saying, "God is looking for those who will look to Him alone as their source of deliverance, rather than to human sources. Those who rely upon God alone in the face of overwhelming distress are viewed by God as loyal."

Trouble and difficulty have a way of surfacing where our true loyalties lie. In times of spiritual conflict, are we loyal to God? And in times of human conflict, are we loyal to our friends?

If Asa had remained loyal to God, he would have experienced a wonderful dimension of God's limitless power. *Loyalty precedes power.* God had victories in mind for Asa beyond his imagination, but he never touched them because he turned elsewhere for help.

### My Personal Stand

As of this writing, I am in personal need of God's delivering power. Specifically, I need deliverance from a physical affliction. My faith is extended to God, but so is my loyalty. In other words, I will look to Him alone until He saves me.

Sometimes you can get relief from human channels. It's always a risk when you turn to human sources, of course, because sometimes you end up worse than when you initially went to them. At best, people can provide you with a little relief. But they cannot save you. Salvation comes from only one source. "'Nor is there salvation in any other, for there is no other name under heaven given among men by which we must be saved'" (Acts 4:12).

Either I look for relief from human channels, or I look for salvation from my God. For me, the answer is clear. My heart is steadfast. I don't just want relief; I want to see the mighty salvation of my God. So I will wait upon Him, looking with dove's eyes to Him alone, until He sends from heaven and saves me.

[16] See 2 Chronicles 16.

### *Loyalty Is Personal*

You must see the intensely personal nature of loyalty. It has everything to do with who. God is loyal to His beloved Son because of who the Son is.

Loyalty makes one's journey with God an intensely personal affair: "God, this is all about You and me. I trust You. I will keep my eyes on You. No man can help me; and no man can hinder me. You are my only source. Now we're in covenant, God, and it's just You and me."

In his youth, David saw his destiny as a very personal matter between him and his God. His perspective was, "Saul is not the blockage here; God is the one blocking my path. My thing is with God. So I will show my loyalty to God by demonstrating a loyal spirit to Saul, and will trust my God to fight for me. He will bring me forth to rich fulfillment." *Because David saw God as the only one directing his destiny, he was able to shake off all temptations to disloyalty.*

If you think that a person can help you, then you'll also believe that a person can hinder you. Once you believe that another human being can hinder your destiny in God, you become susceptible to a spirit of disloyalty, which has its eyes on other people. It is more aware of human dynamics than divine dynamics. Other people are perceived as competitors.

Disloyalty says, "My leader is so _____ [fill in the blank with whatever negative quality]. As long as he's in his position, I'll never be released into my destiny." The next logical step is to do what you can to help your leader move on. "After all," you tell yourself, "I'm doing the leader a favor in nudging him on his way because he could be so much more effective if he just stepped out of his current safety zones." You're sharing in Absalom's spirit and don't even know it. (See the Appendix for a summary of who Absalom was and what he did.)

Absalom, who was disloyal to his father David, led an insurrection to overthrow his father's throne. (We will refer to Absalom repeatedly in this book because he—together with Judas Iscariot—is perhaps the clearest personification of disloyalty in the Bible.) Absalom had a cynical view of his father's agenda. He never believed that his father loved him enough to do right by him. So he concluded that if he was going to get his rightful due, he would have to wrest it himself from his father's hand.

God doesn't want children who relate to Him in this way, who doubt His intentions, and try to use Bible verses to pry from Him what they want for themselves. *God wants true sons who trust Him, who believe in His generosity, and who are convinced that He is committed to their absolute highest and best.* God is bringing to glory many sons and daughters who know what Jesus knew: Even though the pathway may be excruciating at times, God's purpose in the journey is to bring His children forward into their full inheritance until that moment when they stand before all creation as the perfected sons of God.[17]

God is looking for this kind of loyalty, and my soul responds, "Yes, Lord, here is my heart. I am Yours."

### *For Group Discussion*

1.  In what ways have you sensed God looking for loyalty in your heart?

2.  Have you ever perceived another human being as hindering your destiny? How did you get past that?

3.  What is your greatest challenge in seeking to reserve your affections for Christ alone?

4.  Do you feel challenged in any specific ways to look to God alone as your source of deliverance?

---

[17] Romans 8:19.

# CHAPTER 2

# *Honoring Christ's Sphere*

*L* oyalty to God means to me that my affections are reserved solely for Him, and that my eyes are upon Him only as the source of my salvation and help. But it means yet one more thing to me: *Loyalty to God means that I never violate His sphere.*

### *"Sphere" Defined*

To explain that statement, let's begin by looking at Paul's usage of the word "sphere" in this, the only Bible passage where the word is used:

> We, however, will not boast beyond measure, but within the limits of the *sphere* which God appointed us—a *sphere* which especially includes you. For we are not overextending ourselves (as though our authority did not extend to you), for it was to you that we came with the gospel of Christ; not boasting of things beyond measure, that is, in other men's labors, but having hope, that as your faith is increased, we shall be greatly enlarged by you in our *sphere*, to preach the gospel in the regions beyond you, and not to boast in another man's *sphere* of accomplishment (2 Corinthians 10:13-16, italics added).

We see from this passage that Paul's sphere, which was appointed by God, included the Corinthian believers because he came to them first with the gospel. And yet he had authority in their lives only if they voluntarily granted it to him. Paul's hope was that, as their faith increased, they would greatly enlarge his influence and authority in their lives. (It takes faith to give someone more authority in your life.) By so doing, it would release him to take the gospel to "regions beyond."

The word "sphere" is a reference to the measure of influence one exerts in the lives of those within one's circles of exposure. Imagine, for a moment, a rock dropped into a pond. The larger the rock, the larger the ripples it will cause, and the further the ripples will reach. Think of one's sphere like those ripples in a pond. A man's or woman's sphere is the ripple effect that flows out from him or her by virtue of the impact and influence of his or her life and ministry on others.

Each one of us has a sphere of influence we have been given by God,[1] and that sphere will broaden or diminish with the seasons of life. As we mature, our ministry sphere typically broadens. If we have a serious failure before God, He may diminish our sphere for a season. He can also restore whatever sphere has been lost if we repent in a way that moves His heart.

Sphere is a word that describes a horizontal "circle of influence" as opposed to vertical positioning in an organization. It wasn't a title or office that gave Paul his authority with the Corinthians; it was a relational credibility that had been built by virtue of Paul's history with them. Paul had spent 18 months investing in the Corinthian church, so he confidently expressed his conviction that his sphere included them. However, he still appealed to them to enlarge him in his sphere because if they didn't acknowledge that they were within his sphere, his claims were meaningless.

## Christ Has A Sphere

Just as each of us has a sphere, Jesus Christ also has His own sphere. It is His rightful domain which has been given Him from the Father. Christ's sphere is that portion of His inheritance which He shares with none another, and within which His friends constantly seek to enlarge Him.

I want to highlight two primary aspects within Christ's sphere. First is His glory. He has a right to the glory the Father has given Him, and He will not share it with anyone else.[2] The Father's great intention through the drama of human history is that redeemed mankind

---

[1] 2 Corinthians 10:13.
[2] Isaiah 42:8; 48:11.

"should be to the praise of His glory" (Ephesians 1:12). The Father has decreed to the Son, "All the glory is Yours." When the Son is glorified, that's when the Father is glorified.[3] One day the Son will return all glory to the Father, "that God may be all in all" (1 Corinthians 15:28). The Father is not trying to make any other person look good in this entire drama. The only one looking good at the end of the day is to be Jesus Christ. *The glory and the credit are His sphere.*

There is nothing safer for us than when we come away from the thing looking incompetent and weak, and He comes away looking gloriously spectacular in beauty and wisdom.

*A second thing that is within Christ's sphere is the affections of His Bride.* John the Baptist worded it this way, "'He who has the bride is the bridegroom'" (John 3:29). The one who holds the affections of the Bride of Christ in His hand is the heavenly Bridegroom. He possesses her heart, her passions, her desires, her aspirations, her focus, her dreams, her affections. She is His. She is within His sphere, and He will not share her love with anyone else.

### Loyalty To Christ's Sphere

*Loyalty to Christ is intensely aware of His sphere.* The loyal son recognizes that the glory is His, and the affections of the Bride are His, so the loyal son will guard his heart and actions with utmost diligence lest he violate those boundaries. *Disloyalty to Christ is seeking to gain for oneself that which lies exclusively within His sphere.*

A true son is jealous, first of all, over the glory—that none of it come to him. When he starts his day with the prayer, "Hallowed be Your name,"[4] the true son is basically saying, "Lord, may You alone be glorified through everything I say and do today." Loyalty is woven into the very fabric of his prayer life because the true son is jealous for the good reputation of the Lord in all the earth. "Not unto us, O LORD, not unto us, but to Your name give glory, because of Your mercy, because of Your truth" (Psalm 115:1).

There are two primary things that will enamor and impress people, causing them to give glory inordinately to a human vessel: *understanding* and *power*. When we are granted spiritual power to move in signs

---

[3] Philippians 2:11.
[4] Matthew 6:9.

and wonders, men will be in awe, and like Simon the sorcerer[5] will want to acquire this power as well. But there is something even more impressive to men: understanding. When you are granted supernatural understanding into the Kingdom, men will exalt you above measure. Paul was given his thorn in the flesh, not primarily because he was given power, but because he was given understanding. The revelations, even more than the power, wowed the people. Paul had both power and understanding, and it necessitated a thorn in the flesh. God's purpose was to make Paul a pitiful sight to behold so that men would give glory to God rather than to the vessel. How can God give apostolic spheres to vessels without also giving a thorn in the flesh that will deflect the glory away from the vessel?

A true son is jealous over a second thing. *He is jealous over the Bride, that none of her affections be diverted to him, but that they be reserved exclusively for the Bridegroom.* "For I am jealous for you with godly jealousy. For I have betrothed you to one husband, that I may present you as a chaste virgin to Christ" (2 Corinthians 11:2).

Paul was expressing his loyalty to Christ when he wrote, "For we do not preach ourselves, but Christ Jesus the Lord, and ourselves your bondservants for Jesus' sake" (2 Corinthians 4:5). It's so easy to preach Christ while proclaiming ourselves—to preach the gospel of Christ to others, but after we're done the people are talking about us instead of Christ. "What a masterful message! That preacher has an incredible intellect. And what a command of language! I certainly won't forget the day he preached in our church."

The loyal friend is happy after he preaches only if the hearts of God's people are tenderized for their Lord, they are drawn to Him in repentance and intimacy, and they walk away from the meeting talking about how their desire for Christ is stronger than ever. *The loyal friend secures the affections of the Bride for but One—Christ.*

Jesus is intensely loyal to His friends, and He's looking for servants who will be loyal in return by not usurping His sphere. He's looking for true friends who, like John the Baptist, will rejoice when they decrease in the eyes of the people.[6] When Jesus comes to earth the second time, the same thing will happen to Christ's friends that hap-

---

[5] See Acts 8:19 and surrounding verses.
[6] See John 3:26-30.

pened to John the Baptist. The Bride will get her eyes totally off the friend, and onto her Beloved who has returned for her. She will forget the friend's name! She will have eyes only for the Bridegroom, the one who holds her heart in His hand. And the loyal friend, on that day when his years of service to her are totally forgotten, will say, "Now my joy is complete!"

In John the Baptist's parable of John 3:29, there are three personalities represented: Christ ("the bridegroom"), the Lord's servant ("the friend of the bridegroom"), and the people of God ("the bride"). The temptation for the Bride, since the Bridegroom is gone on a long journey, is to get her eyes upon the friend. She begins to become enamored with Christ's friends because she can see them in the flesh (these friends represent leaders in the body of Christ who are called to serve the Bride and prepare her for her wedding day). The true friends of the Bridegroom—the loyal friends—will always resist the temptation to flirt with the Bride. The loyal friends know that if they begin to enjoy and feed off the affections of the Bride, then they are no longer a friend of Christ but a competitor. This is why Christ's true friends are so self-effacing.

Many of the Lord's servants today are praying, "Lord, enlarge my territory! Widen my sphere!"

To some of them the Lord would answer, *"Why should I give you a greater sphere, when you're already violating My sphere with what I've given you?"* I am referring to those servants who have desired to look good in the eyes of people (they've wanted the glory), and those servants who have found their identity in the praises of the Bride (they've found sustenance in the Bride's affections). God Himself will resist their attempts to spread their tent wider.

The greater sphere will be given to the true son—the loyal friend—who is fiercely determined to repudiate any conduct that could come even remotely close to infringing upon Christ's sphere. *When Jesus beholds His true friends who are careful to receive none of the Bride's praises, He will grant to them the apostolic spheres that will garner the great ingathering of the last days, for they will be deemed safe company for the Bride.*

## *For Group Discussion*

1. How could the members of our team grow in honoring each other's spheres of ministry?

2. How do you handle it when the Bride begins to direct her affections to you personally, thanking you for your service?

3. Has the Holy Spirit convicted you of any way in which you have violated Christ's sphere?

# CHAPTER 3

# *What Is Loyalty?*

**B**efore we look more closely at loyalty to God, let's decide what we mean by the word "loyalty." In the briefest language possible, I would describe loyalty as "affectionate allegiance." It is an aligning of our soul with someone else in a familial kind of affection, which could be illustrated by the bond of love that joined David and Jonathan in heart and soul. So for the purposes of our discussion in this book, we'll use "affectionate allegiance" as a concise, descriptive term.

I would like, however, to present a "working definition" of loyalty that is more comprehensive.

## A *Working Definition*

> *Loyalty is a noble, unswerving allegiance, rooted in faith and love, that binds hearts together in common purpose.*

Let's analyze each phrase of this definition. First, we certainly agree that loyalty is "noble." The Creator has written this truth into our conscience. God has placed a "loyalty chip" in the "hard drive" of the human psyche. Every one of us has an innate desire to rise to the nobility of loyalty. We long to have a select group of friends to whom we are loyal, and who in turn are loyal to us. And yet, while we are all capable of this, sin has warped and twisted our fundamental personhood to such an extent that we are now also capable of the opposite. Sometimes our sinfulness drags us down to the quagmires of betrayal and treachery. So much of the pain in our human existence surrounds circumstances where loyalties are broken or violated. Few things are as painful as when a friend whom we thought was true has a change of heart and violates our allegiance. The good news, however, is that through God's grace we can rise to the nobility of Christlikeness.

When the Spirit of God came upon Amasai, he expressed loyalty to David.[1] In contrast, when Satan entered Judas, he plotted to betray Jesus.[2] Can there be any mistaking the origins of loyalty and betrayal? Loyalty is from above, betrayal is from below. Loyalty is noble because it is of God.

According to the second phrase of our working definition, loyalty is unswerving allegiance. *It is allegiance that stands resolutely at the side of one's friend, even in the face of opposing circumstances.* Jonathan was this kind of friend to David. Even when his father, Saul, berated and castigated him for formulating a covenant with David, Jonathan never swerved from his affectionate allegiance. He stood by David, even when he knew it meant he would lose the throne as well as his father's respect. This allegiance made Jonathan one of the greatest examples of loyalty in the Bible.

Next, our definition says that loyalty is "rooted in faith and love." *Loyalty always involves affection or love.* It is a bond of affection that is genuinely gratified when the other is granted greater influence among men, even if it comes at the cost of one's own personal diminishment. Perhaps the other person has done right by you, and now you want to show your gratitude. Whatever the reason for it's affections, loyalty is founded in love. *But loyalty is also founded in faith.* Loyalty believes in the other person. Loyalty will give its heart to David because loyalty believes God fights for David. Where both faith and love are intact, loyalty will remain strong and steadfast.

And finally, we are saying that loyalty "binds hearts together in common purpose." *Loyalty is like glue. It cements us into relationships in a positive way so that our joint partnership in the Gospel accomplishes more than if we were isolated from each other.* Loyalty proves itself with more than just words. It doesn't simply mouth empty assurances of, "I am with you"; it displays itself through proven actions. Jesus said to His disciples, "Do you really love Me? Then lay your lives down for those I love

[1] 1 Chronicles 12:18.
[2] Luke 22:3-4.

by feeding My sheep."[3] Loyalty steps into action, gets harnessed with David, and pulls together for the fulfillment of Kingdom mandates.

### Moving Forward In Purpose

Loyalty is the joining of hands to move forward together in joint exploits. We are given a visual representation of this truth in the life of Jehu, who was anointed by Elisha to be king of Israel. At his anointing he was commissioned to strike down the entire house of King Ahab because of Ahab's wickedness.[4] Anyone loyal to Ahab was to be wiped out.

While Jehu was in the process of fulfilling this word, he met up with his friend, Jehonadab. Jehu called to him, "Is your heart right, as my heart is toward your heart?" Jehonadab answered, "It is." So Jehu replied in this manner: "If it is, give me your hand." The Scripture goes on to say, "So he gave him his hand, and he took him up to him into the chariot" (2 Kings 10:15). Then Jehu said to him, "'Come with me, and see my zeal for the LORD.' So they had him ride in his chariot" (2 Kings 10:16).

*Can you imagine Jehu reaching his hand down, grabbing Jehonadab by the hand, pulling him up into his chariot, and then the two of them riding forth together in common purpose?* This is loyalty.

Furthermore, loyalty will seek a way, if possible, to avoid being separated. We see this so beautifully in Ruth's loyalty to her mother-in-law, Naomi.

> But Ruth said: "Entreat me not to leave you, or to turn back from following after you; for wherever you go, I will go; and wherever you lodge, I will lodge; your people shall be my people, and your God, my God. Where you die, I will die, and there will I be buried. The LORD do so to me, and more also, if anything but death parts you and me" (Ruth 1:16-17).

Loyalty stands at the side of the other and moves forward together. To be loyal to David is to value what he values, to pursue what he pursues, to fight where he fights, and to die where he dies.

---

[3] Paraphrase of John 21:15-17.
[4] 2 Kings 9:7.

### Most People Think They're Loyal

In light of that definition, most of us sincerely believe that we are loyal. While disloyalty is an all-too-common scourge in the church today, we all seem to have the personal conviction that we ourselves are not part of that problem. Aren't we an interesting bunch?

I have never yet met a person who considered himself disloyal. Those who are disloyal usually justify their words and actions, insisting they are standard-bearers of truth. If we could see our disloyalty we would surely stop! It's our blindness that makes it so dangerously insidious.

A friend who is on the pastoral staff of a strong church in America caught my interest when he told the story of a brother in his church who had been loyal for some years, but became disenchanted with the church leaders. The brother ended up leaving the church. Unfortunately, however, he left the church in a disloyal way. Instead of quietly slipping out, he began to speak against the pastor, thus defiling others in the church with his bitterness. A small group picked up his offence and left the church with him. Soon thereafter, this brother was applying for a new job, and on his resumé he had written, "One of my strengths is loyalty." He had just left his church in a flurry of slander but now was claiming loyalty as one of his personal strengths! Like so many, he was blind to his own heart.

*One reason we don't see our disloyalty is that we convince ourselves we are being loyal to something greater.* There is nothing wrong, *per se*, with transferring loyalties from one person to another, or from one group to another. The problem is not in laying aside a working relationship but in *how* we lay it down. Do we do it in a way that is disloyal to one of God's Davids? If the brother in our story had quietly left the church without expressing his discontent to others, he could have maintained his integrity. But because he left with his tongue wagging, he became divisive and disruptive.

*Sometimes disloyalty is loyalty directed at the wrong thing.* Many who are disloyal are actually loyal to no one but themselves. Loyalty to oneself is a very strong deception, however, that we will never be able to see and confess without the Holy Spirit's intervention. In other instances, some are disloyal to David because they've transferred their loyalty to the wrong person—to Absalom. It is of critical importance whom we align ourselves with. Those who join up with Absalom might be loyal, but it's loyalty gone wrong. It will destroy, rather than fulfill, their destiny in God.

At times we may have to choose between two competing allegiances. For example, Jesus said we cannot be loyal to both God and money because they are competing masters.[5] The same principle holds true in the realm of human relationships. You can't be loyal to both David and Saul. *Sometimes being loyal to David means we must sever loyalties to Saul.*

In some scenarios, sides are drawn, and the confrontation comes to a crisis point in which everyone must choose sides. To be loyal is to stand with one's friend when the showdown comes. *Loyalty is that quality that determines with whom you will stand when everyone at the scene must choose a side.*

Look, for example, at Jesus' arrest. There were two groups there in the garden of Gethsemane: The group that stood with Jesus, and the group that stood with the soldiers who came to arrest Jesus. Everyone present was of necessity in one of those two groups. Everyone had to decide where he or she would stand. The Scripture says Judas was found on the side of those arresting Jesus: "Judas, who betrayed Him, also stood with them" (John 18:5). Judas decided with whom he would stand, and it turned out to be an eternal decision.

Although the eleven eventually fled in fear, at least there were those minutes of standing with Jesus when it mattered most. They crumpled under pressure, but even so they refused to stand with the arresters. And because of it, Jesus told Mary after His resurrection that they were His "brethren," and that He desired to meet with them.[6] He owned them because they owned Him.

### Amasai's Expression Of Loyalty

The Bible's clearest utterance of loyalty is to be found in the pages of David's history, at a time when he was still an outcast from his people:

Then some of the sons of Benjamin and Judah came to David

[5] Luke 16:13.
[6] Matthew 28:10; John 20:17.

at the stronghold. And David went out to meet them, and answered and said to them, "If you have come peaceably to me to help me, my heart will be united with you; but if to betray me to my enemies, since there is no wrong in my hands, may the God of our fathers look and bring judgment." Then the Spirit came upon Amasai, chief of the captains, and he said: "We are yours, O David; we are on your side, O son of Jesse! Peace, peace to you, and peace to your helpers! For your God helps you." So David received them, and made them captains of the troop (1 Chronicles 12:16-18).

Since King Saul was a Benjamite, the "sons of Benjamin" who came to David on this occasion would have been Saul's relatives. Members of the same tribe would naturally stick together, so Saul's most ardent supporters were Benjamites. But now here came some of Saul's relatives to David, expressing their interest to join up with him.

David wasn't sure if their coming to him was in pretense or sincerity, so his greeting to them was somewhat guarded. He was basically saying, "If you have come as relatives of Saul to betray me to him, then may the God of our fathers look and bring judgment against you."

Some of the men in the party coming to David were also relatives of David (of the tribe of Judah). One of them, a leader in their midst named Amasai, received a sudden rush of Holy Spirit anointing on his life, and replied to David with words that were born in the heart of God: "We are yours, O David; we are on your side, O son of Jesse! Peace, peace to you, and peace to your helpers! For your God helps you."

This utterance of loyalty is fantastic and thrilling. Amasai was swept up by the Spirit's passions and expressed the kind of loyalty that only God can give. He was saying, "Your wish is our command because our hearts have been joined to you by God." Amasai wasn't saying, "Let us know what you'd like, David, and then we'll pray about it and get back to you and let you know whether or not we'll do what you're asking." He offered no qualifiers. There was no reservation nor self-preservation, nor provision for a quiet exit if things didn't work out as planned. None of that. God had produced a holy loyalty in their hearts toward God's anointed man, and Amasai was empowered by the Spirit to express their intentions with heartfelt sincerity.

The Spirit's role in their loyalty testifies that *this is a holy and noble subject we're handling. True loyalty is impossible apart from the Spirit's help.* When motives are upright, I believe the Holy Spirit loves to rush in and impart this kind of loyalty to God's Davids.

Amasai models the kind of loyalty that is willing to suffer loss or personal diminishment for the sake of promoting David's cause. These men were putting their lives on the line in order to support David. Loyalty to God works the same way. *The loyal servant of the Lord lays his life down for the furtherance of God's interests.*

Sometimes loyalty will involve a pledge, like Amasai's pledge of fidelity to David. You will notice that David did not require or solicit Amasai's pledge; it was totally voluntary on Amasai's part. *Loyalty must be voluntary, for as soon as it is coerced, required, or demanded, it ceases to be authentic and becomes more like a militaristic imposition of adherence.*

At first, David was guarded because he knew that some of Saul's relatives were in the group. But once they all pledged their affectionate allegiance to him, David's acceptance of them was implicit and immediate. All they had to say was, "We are yours," and David believed the best in them. He didn't take them through a grueling interview to be sure their motives were noble. He accepted and received them all— even the evil ones. In other words, *he didn't have a filtering mechanism to protect himself against betrayal.*

So what was David's contingency plan to protect himself against those who might betray him? He called on God in their presence, for God to see and judge. *If David was to be protected from betrayal, God Himself would have to do it.*

### The Power Of Princes

The princes of the land always have the power to influence others. Amasai had the ability, as a chief among captains, to use his influence either for or against David's cause. Because of his noble heart, Amasai went down in the chronicles of sacred literature as the man who used his influence to inspire others to be loyal to David. God give us more Amasais!

*Princes and elders often become lightning rods for those who are discontent with the king* (the primary leader). The malcontents will approach an elder or prince with clever language to discern whether the prince or elder is sympathetic to their grievance. When a prince says, "Well, let's just pray for the leader—because after all, he is human, you know," that prince just blew it. That response says, "Well, you're right; but we can't change the king's mind." So the malcontent immediately knows he has an ally in this prince. If the elder or prince is loyal to David, however, he will use his influence to put out the fires of discontentment in David's ranks.

Ahithophel was a brilliant man who was one of David's chief advisors and an eminent elder in the land. Had he been loyal to David, he could have averted the tragedy of Absalom's treason. When Absalom met with him secretly, Ahithophel could have used his influence to turn Absalom's heart; instead, he was infected by Absalom's offence. The Bible doesn't tell us when the rendezvous happened, but Absalom came to see if he could find an ally in Ahithophel. Absalom was constantly on the lookout to find those who might have an unresolved grievance toward his father, King David, so that he could win them over to his insurrection. On the surface it would appear totally understandable that Absalom would choose such a trustworthy friend of David's with whom to vent his frustrations and pour out his grievances. But because of his disloyalty, Absalom wasn't coming for help to process his thoughts; rather, he was coming to incite dissension in Ahithophel's heart. But he had to do it very shrewdly.

Knowing that Ahithophel was Bathsheba's grandfather,[7] Absalom most likely sought to determine if Ahithophel might still be slightly bitter toward David for the way David had violated his granddaughter, Bathsheba, and murdered her husband. Left alone, Ahithophel's grievance would have probably simmered down into a quiet death. But Absalom came and blew on the cooling embers, and found a way to resurrect in Ahithophel's heart a grudge that had been almost forgotten. *This is standard procedure for disloyal sons—they will go to the elders of the land and see if they can gain a co-conspirator.* As Absalom plied him with questions, Ahithophel realized that here was a man who had the charisma, bearing, and brainpower to actually pull off a coup. Suddenly, Ahithophel found himself with a win-win scenario in which he could have revenge on the man who violated his granddaughter, while

[7] 2 Samuel 11:3; 23:34.

at the same time remain in his position of influence at the side of the king of Israel (the new king, that is—Absalom). In whatever manner the conversation actually transpired, Absalom came away with an ally.[8]

Herein is the difference between Absalom and Amasai: Absalom used his influence to turn others against David; Amasai used his influence to turn others toward David in loving loyalty.

### For Group Discussion

1. Can you think of ways to improve upon this book's working definition of loyalty?
2. Talk about loyalty as glue. What does that image bring to mind, especially as it relates to your group or team?
3. What are some ways we might be blind to areas of disloyalty in our hearts?
4. Tell about the time you had to choose between two loyalties.
5. Talk about Amasai's expression of loyalty. Could you imagine saying something similar to your leader?
6. How should we respond if someone comes to us with a complaint or criticism about our leader?

[8] 2 Samuel 15:12.

# CHAPTER 4

## *What's The Big Deal About Loyalty Anyways?*

*I*s the topic of loyalty really all that important? Or are we making a bigger deal out of it than it deserves? I mean, is loyalty *that* important to God?

Answer: The subject of loyalty is *massively* important in the eyes of God. Nothing gains greater importance among God's core values. One main reason for the primacy of this subject is the fact that it was disloyalty that disrupted heaven's unity and joy. Once you've experienced it, disloyalty becomes unforgettable. Disloyalty, fueled by pride, was the catalyst for Lucifer's rebellion and fall. It fractured eternity in two, introducing into a universe of light something never before seen—the realm of darkness. Never before had God's benevolent heart been so violated and scorned. It was the most painful confrontation God had ever endured. That's why issues of loyalty run deep in God's heart and history.

God's redemptive plan is being carried out on a demon-ridden planet—on Satan's turf, under Satan's house rules. Why? Because God is preparing a Bride for His Son who, having said, "Yes," under the greatest pressures, will never turn her back on her Lord as did Lucifer. Throughout the eons of Glory, she will remain eternally true to the nail-scarred One because of the battle she overcame to obtain eternal life.

To understand all this better, let's look at the circumstances surrounding Lucifer's fall.

### Lucifer's Disloyalty

Lucifer was one of God's most powerful angels whom God exalted with incredible glory and honor.[1] God chose to lavish amazing kindness and goodness upon Lucifer. He was so stunning in beauty and impressive in power that he was held in honor by heaven's hosts. But Lucifer's exalted state went to his head, and he began to be filled with pride.[2] God had given Lucifer such incredible glory that when he decided to lead an insurrection against God's throne, he was able by the power of his beauty and splendor to sway fully a third of heaven's angels to his side.[3] His massive powers must have been truly impressive! But he was no match for God. When everything shook down, Lucifer and his cohorts were overthrown and cast from heaven to the earth.

It's almost unthinkable, but it really happened: There was a coup in heaven! Lucifer became disgruntled with God and eventually tried to destroy Him. You might wonder, "How could anyone get mad at God? He's perfect!" True, He's perfect in all His ways; but even the perfect God had a third of His angels turn against Him.

So I suppose it should not surprise us when others are disloyal to us, considering our weaknesses and foibles and faults. Sometimes others are disloyal to us even when we handle them perfectly. *If God who is altogether beautiful incurred the hate of Lucifer, and if Jesus whose leadership is perfect incurred the betrayal of one of His disciples, then little wonder today's Davids find people around them wanting to throw off their yoke of leadership.*

### How Did He Do It?

I've often wondered how Lucifer could have pulled off an insurrection against God within the domain of God's glory. How could he get away with it? The only reasonable answer is that God *allowed* Lucifer to organize his coup. God saw the rebellion in its inception, He watched while it grew, and then He expelled Satan when it reached full manifestation.

It's fascinating to consider that God did nothing to stop Lucifer while he was enlisting recruits from among heaven's hosts. God was

[1] Isaiah 14:9-17; Ezekiel 28:12-19.
[2] Isaiah 14:13-14.
[3] Revelation 12:4.

26

aware of the amassing of the malcontents, and yet He refused to intervene while more and more angels were being drawn into Lucifer's convoluted thinking. Why was God silent when He could have snuffed out the rebellion in its infancy? The answer is found in God's desire for true loyalty. *God doesn't want subjects who are loyal to Him because He has sealed off all other options.* No, He wants those who, despite alternatives, willfully choose Him. If the angels wanted to be loyal to Lucifer, God would do nothing to stop them.

Intriguingly, David chose the same approach in relating to his disloyal son, Absalom. He knew Absalom was critical of his leadership and that he was drawing the affections of the Israelites to himself. And yet David did nothing to stop Absalom's insurrection while it was in its formative stages. *David's example teaches us that, even today, the wise leader may choose to not interfere with or stop the son who is spreading bitterness and drawing followers to himself. The heart of the true father is always to give the son the benefit of the doubt, giving him room to come to his senses.* Spiritual fathers conduct themselves in this manner because they desire to be like their heavenly Father.

### Why Did He Do It?

The next question I've had is, why did Lucifer get a bad attitude toward God? I have not been able to find a clear answer to that question in the Bible; I do, however, have some personal opinions that are based upon my understanding of God's ways. Realizing that we're in an area of conjecture, I'll share my best guess at why Lucifer turned against God.

A beginning hint appears for us in Hebrews 12:9, "Furthermore, we have had human fathers who corrected us, and we paid them respect. Shall we not much more readily be in subjection to the Father of spirits and live?" As the Father of spirits, God was Lucifer's Father from the beginning. He would have reserved the right to discipline Lucifer and father him as He deemed most fitting. And I think that's where it may have gone bad. It's possible Lucifer became offended at God's fathering style. I'm suggesting there came a point at which Lucifer chafed at God's disciplines.

I've often wondered if God might have asked something of Lucifer somewhat akin to what He asked of His own Son. God has a way of calling His beloved ones to crushing and crucifixion. Did God perhaps call Lucifer to something that Lucifer thought was unfair, overly harsh, or oppressive? He may have pointed to God's assignment and said to heaven's angels, "What kind of a leader assigns to His followers this kind of pathway? A tyrant! This is wrong! How can we say God is good when He requires this kind of sacrifice from His creatures?"

We don't know the exact nature of Lucifer's grievance, but it caused him to question and impugn the goodness of God. Lucifer no doubt began slandering God as being an onerous, controlling, self-serving despot. Whatever God might have asked of Lucifer, a third of heaven's angels looked at the assignment and agreed with Lucifer's protest. They took on Lucifer's offence and basically said to God, "If this is how You're going to run Your kingdom, we stand with Lucifer in registering a formal complaint."

Every father has the right to distribute his inheritance to his sons in his own time and way. God had his own way of bringing Lucifer into his destiny, but Lucifer didn't like God's plan.

Perhaps Lucifer—who has now become Satan—was able to garner the loyalty of a third of heaven's angels by offering them grandiose promises. By disowning God, these angels ended up with Satan as their father. But they likely didn't know what they were getting. As long as Lucifer was in Father God's house, the covering of God's house kept the issues in Lucifer's heart suppressed. But once he was ousted from heaven and removed from any restraining forces, the full darkness of Satan's treacherous heart was manifested. He came to embody every-thing that God was not.

### The Crucial Nature Of Loyalty

When Lucifer chose to be loyal to himself, it was the most impor-tant decision he ever made. When Absalom and Judas Iscariot made the same decision, it determined their eternal destiny. The issues at stake are enormous, a truth that is also seen so grippingly in the life of Pontius Pilate.

At Jesus' trial, the chief priests tried every conceivable argument to convince Pilate to deliver Jesus up to death. They started off by sug-gesting that Jesus was organizing a political movement to overthrow the powers of Rome. They claimed He was preparing to overthrow

Rome and establish Himself as King in the nation.[4] But Pilate studied Jesus' responses and didn't buy it.

Their second accusation was that Jesus was guilty of blasphemy by claiming to be the Son of God.[5] This accusation unnerved Pilate, especially since Jesus didn't strike him as delusional. But it wasn't enough for him to pass sentence.

Then the chief priests pulled out their ace of spades. They made Jesus' trial an issue of loyalties.

> From then on Pilate sought to release Him, but the Jews cried out, saying, "If you let this Man go, you are not Caesar's friend. Whoever makes himself a king speaks against Caesar." When Pilate therefore heard that saying, he brought Jesus out and sat down in the judgment seat in a place that is called The Pavement, but in Hebrew, Gabbatha...Then he delivered Him to them to be crucified."[6]

The Jews were asking Pilate, "Whose friend are you? Caesar's, or Jesus's?" They were saying, "Pilate, you've got to decide who you're going to be loyal to. You can't be loyal to both Jesus of Nazareth and Caesar. So which is it? Jesus? Or Caesar?"

When they made it an issue of loyalties, Pilate didn't hesitate another moment. For him, there was no question. He was not going to align himself with this Jewish crusader who didn't have enough sense to keep His nose out of trouble. No, he was with Caesar. Since Pilate was being forced to choose sides, Jesus would have to die.

It looked like Jesus was on trial before Pilate, when in fact Pilate was on trial before Jesus.

Pilate aligned his loyalty with Caesar, and crucified the Lord of Glory—a decision that determined his eternal destiny. Here's the powerful truth Pilate's terrible decision illustrates: *Where you choose to place your loyalty may be the most important decision of your entire lifetime.*

---

[4] This is basically the issue underlying John 18:33.
[5] John 19:7-8.
[6] John 19:12-13,16.

### *For Group Discussion*

1. How important is the topic of loyalty to you?
2. What stood out most to you, regarding Lucifer's rebellion against God?
3. Do you agree with the author's supposition that Lucifer became offended at God's fathering and discipline?
4. Is there any kind of loyalty decision before you right now? Tell us about it.

# CHAPTER 5

# Satan: Purveyor of Disloyalty

Satan (whose name means Accuser) is now on a mission among mankind to incite further disloyalty to God. He accuses God to us, tempting us to turn against God. The caricatures he paints of God's character are distortions of the truth intended to get us offended at God. Satan's role as the purveyor of disloyalty is as ancient as human history and goes all the way back to the first book of the Bible.

Scripture is launched with the subject of loyalty. The book of Job was the first Bible book actually put on paper (preceding the book of Genesis in antiquity), and the primary theme of the book is loyalty. The book of Job is the fascinating saga of a man who was being disciplined by his Father God, with the primary issue being whether that man, in his horrendous distress, would remain loyal to God, and whether his friends would remain loyal to him during the journey.

God actually started the fight by pointing out Job to Satan. "Then the LORD said to Satan, 'Have you considered My servant Job, that there is none like him on the earth, a blameless and upright man, one who fears God and shuns evil?'" (Job 1:8). God was extolling Job's loyalty. Satan couldn't listen to such words in silence, so he shot back his accusations.

Satan's accusation against God could be paraphrased something like this: "God, You gain the loyalty of man's affections with gifts. You're buying Job's love. But it's not true loyalty. Job isn't loyal to *You*; He's loyal to Your *generosity*. He's loyal to You because You're so rich. And I'll prove it to You, if You'll give me the chance. All I ask is that

You remove Your gifts from his life, and then let's take another look. Take Your kindness away from him, and You'll see how real Job's loyalty is. Touch his possessions, and I bet he'll curse You to Your face!"

The fact that Job's loyalty was proven true has not stopped the Accuser. He continues to assault those who are loyal to God. He attempts to prove that man's loyalty to God is shallow, and he *hates* it when he is proven wrong by another Job-like saint. He is tormented in his soul when he sees men and women giving to God the loyalty he once gave.[1]

### Satan's Offer To Jesus

Like everyone else, Jesus also had to pass the loyalty test. When Jesus came to earth in a human body, He was accosted at age 30 by Satan who tried to trick Him into forfeiting His inheritance through subtle temptations. Each temptation was tailored to appeal to valid desires within Christ's heart, but then to entice Him to act upon those desires in a wrong way.

Of the three main temptations Jesus faced, one is especially relevant to our topic.

> Then the devil, taking Him up on a high mountain, showed Him all the kingdoms of the world in a moment of time. And the devil said to Him, "All this authority I will give You, and their glory; for this has been delivered to me, and I give it to whomever I wish. Therefore, if You will worship before me, all will be Yours." And Jesus answered and said to him, "Get behind Me, Satan! For it is written, 'You shall worship the LORD your God, and Him only you shall serve'" (Luke 4:5-8).

Satan was offering Jesus that which was His rightful inheritance—the kingdoms of the world—and He could get them the easy way by simply worshiping him. Satan was telling Jesus that He could get His rightful due an easier way than by going through the agony of the cross. By simply bowing the knee, Jesus could have everything He had come to earth for, and He could have it immediately.

In essence, Satan was attacking God's fathering style. He was ba-

---

[1] For further reflection see, Pain, Perplexity, and Promotion: A prophetic interpretation of the book of Job, available at www.oasishouse.net. It's a passionate book with a gripping message on the relevance of Job's life for today.

sically saying, "It's tyrannical of Your Father to call You to death and crucifixion when You've done nothing to deserve it. If You were to accept me as Your father, I would father You so much better. In fact, I would give You everything Your Father is offering You, and all I ask is that You simply love me. All I want is Your love. But that's not good enough for Your heavenly Father; He still wants You to suffer. But it's enough to me if You'll love me. Just love and worship me and receive me as Your father, and I'll give You Your inheritance in the dignified way You deserve."

Satan's offer was nothing but empty lies, however, and Jesus knew it. He refused to renounce His loyalty to His heavenly Father. He would not bow to Satan, not even under pressure. When called to lay down his life, Lucifer had refused and turned from God. Now the Father was calling on Jesus to lay down His life, and Satan was tempting Him to respond as he had.

Satan was disloyal to God, but He could not persuade Jesus to join him. Nevertheless, Satan's disloyalty has been a source of great distress and pain to God. God had given him so much! The descriptions of Ezekiel 28 would seem to hint that God favored Lucifer with more glory and honor than any other angel. It seems that God withheld nothing from Lucifer but the throne itself. And yet that's what Lucifer wanted. *Lucifer's rebellion was intensely painful to God, and it set God's heart to searching out how He could bestow glory upon His creation without it turning against Him.*

### Lucifer Replaced

God's unhappy history with Lucifer became the backdrop against which God conceived of redemption's plan for mankind. He wanted to produce a creation upon which He could safely lavish the full extent of His affections and glory, but which would never rise up in pride and disloyalty like Lucifer did. How could He produce such a creation? The answer was found in allowing them to be birthed into willful disloyalty but then wooing them to a place of voluntary loyalty.

Through sin, man has been born into brokenness, heartache, despair, and torment. Jesus came to save us from our lost condition and bring us into heaven's courts. God strategically designed a salvation that would produce within redeemed men and women a never-ending heart of affectionate allegiance for the One who would rescue them from darkness and despair. Oh, the wonder of voluntary love, given freely from the hearts of weak, broken, poor people!

We have tasted the devastating fruit of disloyalty, and we have also tasted the glorious joy of loving loyalty given freely to our Savior and Friend. Having drunk the gall of disloyalty, redeemed man will never again rise in insurrection against God. Our loyalty will be pure and everlasting. We will be His forever! We will be eternally loyal to our Bridegroom because He has captured our hearts through love.

Some of the strongest verses in the Bible are directed to believers who give their loyalty to Christ, but then betray His love and turn away in disloyalty.[2] That's because God has been so loyal to you—sacrificing His Son on Calvary, receiving none of the enemy's accusations against you, and allowing no one to pluck you out of His hand—and now He demands loyalty in return. God has no place for disloyalty in His heaven.

God has known the incalculable pain of having a third of heaven's angels turn against Him in disloyalty. But now He is preparing a joy beyond all joys—a fallen creation that is being prepared as a Bride who will forever give her voluntary, undying love to her Beloved.

"The heart knows its own bitterness, and a stranger does not share its joy" (Proverbs 14:10). No one but you really knows the inner bitterness of your private pain. The same is true for God. No one really knows the bitterness of soul that God has experienced over the fall of Lucifer and the disloyalty of Lucifer's angels. But it's equally true that we also do not yet know the joy of God's heart over the redeemed children who are now coming into His family. No stranger will ever know this joy of God's heart. But you are no stranger; you're family! When God's redemptive purposes are fulfilled, you and I will step into the magnificent joy of God's heart over a completed household that has been joined together, forever, in affectionate allegiance. We have no idea the riches of the glory and goodness that God has prepared for those who love Him! Hallelujah!

---

[2] See Hebrews 6:4-6; 10:26-31.

## For Group Discussion

1. Talk about your understanding of Job's life, since loyalty is the main issue in that book.
2. How does Christ's loyalty to the Father challenge you, especially considering that it involved crucifixion?
3. Do you feel like you could still be tempted to turn away from your loyalty to Christ?

# CHAPTER 6

## *God Makes A Great Friend*

**W**hen you place your faith in the Gospel of Jesus Christ and set your love upon Jesus your Redeemer, something powerful takes place in the heavenlies: God takes the fiery loyalty He has for His Son and transfers it to you. Jesus testified of this, "'For the Father Himself loves you, because you have loved Me, and have believed that I came forth from God.'"[1]

His loyalty is so firm and His grip on your life so steadfast that no one can snatch you out of your Father's hand.[2] He sings over you, "'Yes, I have loved you with an everlasting love'" (Jeremiah 31:3). And He adds, "'I will never leave you nor forsake you'" (Hebrews 13:5). Celebrate and revel in this truth: *God is loyal to you, empowering you to be loyal to Him!*

Redemption's story is all about loyalty:

- The Father is loyal to the Son.
- The Son has surrendered His life unto death in allegiance to the Father.
- When men and women express faith in Christ, they give their hearts in fidelity to Christ.
- The Father gives to redeemed men and women the same loyalty He gives His own Son.

### *You Want God For A Friend!*

Needing a friend? God makes a great friend. He really does! When

[1] John 16:27; see also John 12:26; 14:21; 17:23.
[2] John 10:29.

you become His friend, you possess the most valuable thing in the universe—the loyalty of God.

One man who had this was David, and many generations were blessed as a result. There were times when God was inclined to judge the people because of their sinfulness, but then He would remember His covenant with David and relent.[3] God basically said to the people, "The only reason you're being blessed right now is because of my loyalty to David."

God honored His loyalty to Abraham in the same way. God told successive generations that He would be with them and bless them specifically because He was maintaining His loyalty to His friend, Abraham.[4] *The point here is that when God is loyal to you, He gives you a spiritual inheritance in every successive generation.*

There's one story in particular about Abraham that demonstrates God's unusual loyalty to His friends. It actually happened at a time when his name was still Abram. Abram was afraid that the king of the land, Abimilech, would see how beautiful his wife was and kill him in order to marry her. So Abram told his wife, Sarai, that she should claim to be his sister in order to preserve his life, which Sarai agreed to do.[5] When Abimilech laid eyes on her and heard she was Abram's sister, he immediately took her into his house and began preparations to bring her into his harem.

But God came to Abimelech in a dream and said, "You're a dead man—you've taken another man's wife into your house."[6]

Abimelech replied, "Lord, is it Your practice to go around killing entire nations of righteous people? I haven't so much as touched the woman."

The Lord said, "You're dead."

Abimelech immediately remonstrated, "But Lord, he told me she was his sister, and she herself said the same thing."

The Lord said, "You're dead."

Abimelech came back, "Lord, I did this thing in total integrity and

---

[3] See 1 Kings 11:12-13, 36; 2 Kings 8:19; 20:6.
[4] See Genesis 26:3-5, 24; Exodus 2:24; Psalm 105:42.
[5] See Genesis 20.
[6] See Genesis 20:4.

with innocent hands!"

"Yes, I know," came the answer. "But the man's a prophet. So restore his wife to him, or you shall surely die, along with all who are yours."

In my mind I'm thinking, "Lord, aren't You being a little hard on Abimelech? I mean, Abram is the one who has blown it here. Abram is the one who has lied and cowered in fear. Abimelech is the good guy in the story. So why did You come down so hard on Abimelech?"

I can imagine the Lord's answer, "Because Abram is my friend. I know Him, and he knows Me. I always stick by My friends."

God was loyal to Abram *even when Abram was wrong.*

If this is the kind of loyalty that flows in God's heart, then I want Him to be loyal to me, too. Because I need a God who will be my Friend even when I make foolish mistakes (which is often enough).

This is the God who has won my loyalties.

### *For Group Discussion*

1. What does it mean to you, to be a friend of God?
2. How does His grace and loyalty comfort you and make you feel secure in His love?
3. What kinds of feelings or thoughts does the Abraham story evoke within you?

# CHAPTER 7

# *Character Qualities God Promotes*

One reason we want to be loyal to God is because He rewards loyalty with greater responsibility. In fact, there are several character qualities that are especially important to God. Loyalty is just one of them. *When God finds a vessel that is walking before Him in integrity, He promotes that servant to places of nobler responsibility and deeper servanthood.*

Serve a little bit, He'll give you greater ways to serve. Handle properly what He's given you and He'll give you more. "'For to everyone who has, more will be given, and he will have abundance'"(Matthew 25:29).

When God considers which vessels might be entrusted with greater spheres of servanthood, He does not look for sincerity, or for passion or giftedness or education. He looks rather for *character*. The great issue before God is whether the vessel has evidenced *growth of character*. Is this person becoming more like Jesus? Is this person increasingly manifesting the character qualities of Christ? When the answer is yes, God will take that person to the next level of testing and inner development.

By looking at Psalm 101, we can discover the character qualities God is looking for.

### A Psalm About Leadership Criteria

In this Psalm, David will itemize the qualities he looks for in choosing leaders.

> Whoever secretly slanders his neighbor, him I will destroy; the one who has a haughty look and a proud heart, him I will not endure. My eyes shall be on the faithful of the land, that they may dwell with me; he who walks in a perfect way, he shall serve me. He who works deceit shall not dwell within my house; he who tells lies shall not continue in my presence (Psalm 101:5-7).

David is speaking of those he invites into his presence, or into his home—that is, into his inner circle of leadership. David is basically saying, "These are the character qualities I look for as I build my leadership team. When I need to appoint someone to a place of service, let me tell you the kind of person I'm looking for."

Someone might ask, "Isn't it sort of strange to write a worship song about criteria for choosing leaders?" True, it's not the kind of lyrical prose you'd expect to find in today's worship songs. Keep in mind, though, that the songs of that day were used as one of the primary methods for teaching children and adults the truths of the covenant. They didn't have books and textbooks as we have today, so most instruction was conveyed orally through poetry, songs, and rote memorization. David felt strongly enough about leadership qualifications that he wanted these themes to be remembered throughout the generations.

### David's Top Five Leadership Criteria

I see at least five character qualities David valued in the lives of those on his leadership team: Loyalty, humility, faithfulness, uprightness, and truthfulness. Let's look at them individually.

### Loyalty

Whoever secretly slanders his neighbor, him I will destroy (verse 5a).

While David doesn't use the word "loyalty" here, he talks the language of loyalty. The one who slanders his neighbor is one who is not loyal in his earthly relationships. The loyal friend does not stoop to slander. Rather, he does all in his power to promote the good reputation of his friend. David begins his list by saying he will not tolerate the overt disloyalty of slander among his leaders.

In raising issues of loyalty first, it's obvious that it was a very important quality to David. His own experiences had taught him the value of loyalty. While serving under Saul, he had learned that it wasn't enough to be a giant killer and the theme of maidens' songs. Even though he had given his strength for the sake of the people and had been a mighty deliverer for them, they had still plotted together with Saul against his life.

No, strength and ability were not enough. Above all, David wanted loyalty on his leadership team.

### Humility

The one who has a haughty look and a proud heart, him I will not endure (verse 5b).

David was hesitant to bring into leadership positions those who carried themselves in a way that conveyed a haughty attitude.

God also has the practice of promoting humility. Scripture says, "'God resists the proud, but gives grace to the humble.' Therefore humble yourselves under the mighty hand of God, that He may exalt you in due time" (1 Peter 5:5-6). When we embrace humility, we qualify to be exalted "in due time." Humble people have ownership of Christ's words, "Without Me you can do nothing." They realize that no matter how strong their giftings and talents, all their labors are of no effect if God isn't building the house.

If you're a leader, develop a nose for humility. Notice when it's absent, and notice when it's present. When you see arrogance in one of the servants, don't shrug it off as an insignificant thing. Pride should never be promoted. When you've discerned a member of your team who is truly humble, you have found a vessel that is safe to promote to higher responsibilities. *Don't make the mistake of thinking that promotion will help the vessel to learn humility.* Make sure the humility is there first. If God waits to see humility before promoting someone, then we should too.

### Faithfulness

My eyes shall be on the faithful of the land, that they may dwell with me (verse 6a).

David was on the lookout for faithfulness, and wise leaders today will do likewise. Is the person faithful to execute small details with diligence and accuracy? Is she a woman of her word? Does he follow through to full completion without having to be monitored? We don't need people who think they are God's gift to humanity; we need people who will serve diligently and faithfully.

God promotes faithfulness. When He sees a servant that is faithful and diligent to fulfill all his responsibilities, God says to that faithful servant, "'You were faithful over a few things, I will make you ruler over many things'" (Matthew 25:21). In other words, God promotes faithfulness to higher levels of responsibility.

If God does that, leaders should also promote those who are most faithful on the team. *Don't promote mere talent; promote faithfulness.* Develop an eye for faithfulness. When you see it, mark it. You're probably looking at a servant that will be promoted in time to an even greater servanthood.

## Uprightness

**He who walks in a perfect way, he shall serve me (verse 6b).**

Here David is pointing to the character quality of godliness or blamelessness. A man had to walk in a manner of life that was above reproach in others' eyes before David would bring him into his inner circle.

God feels the same way. He also promotes uprightness. God is holy and true (Revelation 6:10), and when He sees people who are holy and true, He brings them into the immediacy of His presence and promotes them to greater spheres of service. Godliness is an essential qualification for leadership. Never promote someone without it.

## Truthfulness

**He who works deceit shall not dwell within my house; he who tells lies shall not continue in my presence (verse 7).**

Honesty is an absolutely essential quality for leaders to demonstrate. No lie is a small lie. David himself had done some lying in his history, but he learned that it never secured God's favor. Now, he wanted men of integrity on his team—men who would speak the truth.

David wanted those who would serve him in his royal court to evidence these five character qualities. One reason might be that David recognized these were the kinds of character qualities that God Himself desired before His throne. In Psalm 15, David wrote about the character of the person God invites into *His* inner circle.

> LORD, who may abide in Your tabernacle? Who may dwell in Your holy hill? He who walks uprightly, and works righteousness, and speaks the truth in his heart; he who does not backbite with his tongue, nor does evil to his neighbor, nor does he take up a reproach against his friend (Psalm 15:1-3).

### God Promotes Loyalty

Whom does God promote to the place of abiding in His presence? Psalm 15:3 says God brings into His immediate presence the man who does not "take up a reproach against his friend." That phrase is describing a loyal person. One who is loyal to his friend will not be quick to pick up an accusation or reproach against his friend because he knows him. The loyal spirit will say, "No, that can't be right. I know John. He doesn't conduct himself that way. John is my friend, and I know he would never intentionally do the kind of thing you're saying he has done." *A loyal person will not take up an offence or reproach against his or her friend because loyalty puts more weight in the integrity of the friend than in the credibility of the accusation.* To the loyal friend, the burden of proof is with the accuser. Unless the accuser can present sufficiently compelling evidence, the reproach is dismissed because of the relationship that loyalty has built. And even if the accusation proves to be true, the true friend confronts and searches out the truth in loyalty and love.

An important part of being a good friend is being loyal. David was asserting that *God promotes into His inner circle those who are loyal to their human friends.* The Lord seems to think that the one who is loyal to his friend on earth will be loyal, in like manner, to his heavenly Friend.

*God earmarks the loyal for promotion.* "'For the eyes of the LORD run to and fro throughout the whole earth, to show Himself strong on

*45*

behalf of those whose heart is loyal to Him'" (2 Chronicles 16:9). God is always searching the world over for servants who are truly loyal to Him. When He finds that kind of loving loyalty, He raises them up and shows Himself strong on their behalf. The wise leader will take his cue from God's leadership style and will wait to promote someone until he sees enduring qualities like faithfulness, humility, and loyalty in the life of that member.

Take a lesson from Korah. Korah wanted to be promoted by God to the place that Aaron or Moses held over the people. But God would not promote Korah because he was loyal only to himself. If Korah had been the leader, and God had said to him, "Korah, step aside, I'm going to destroy the entire nation of Israel, and raise up another nation through you," Korah would have accepted the offer. He would have said, "Here am I, Lord, Your faithful servant; let it be done to me according to Your word." But God didn't need that kind of a man as leader. He needed a loyal man like Moses who, when God spoke of destroying the nation, would stand in the breach and turn away the wrath of God.[1] *The disloyal servant will never be the intercessor God needs, so he will not be promoted by God.*

Look for loyalty in those whom you promote to your primary levels of leadership. You may not enjoy the luxury of having loyalty among all those who serve in secondary or tertiary levels of leadership, but it is critical that those in your inner core of leadership be loyal in love to you.

Others who don't understand this leadership principle may find your selection of primary leaders to be exclusive and smacking of favoritism. But wise leaders have come to learn that we shouldn't promote someone simply because he or she has tenure and influence in the system. Tenure does not guarantee loyalty. So a wise leader may choose to promote a loyal person with less experience over someone who has institutional seniority but who lacks a true heart of loyalty.

I'd like to close this chapter with a contemporary example of someone who has been promoted because of loyalty, and Larry Hill comes to mind. A friend showed me a letter he had received from Dr. Larry Hill, Executive Director of Christ For The Nations Institute in Dallas,

---

[1] Psalm 106:23.

TX, inviting him to come speak on their campus once again. Larry wrote to my friend, "The Guest Speaker Committee, and the Lindsay family, would love for you to come back to CFNI and minister to our students." I was struck by how Larry referenced "the Lindsay family" in his letter. Christ For The Nations was founded by Gordon and Freda Lindsay, and is led today by Mom Lindsay and her son, Dennis Lindsay. Larry was honoring their legacy and leadership in his letter. Larry is a powerful minister of the gospel in his own right, and would not need to follow in the shadow of the Lindsays in order to establish his own ministry platform. But he is honoring of the fact that he stands in a place of entrustment given to him by the Lindsays. Even a simple letter of invitation was reflective of his personal loyalty to them. Because of that loyalty, he is trusted to serve as the primary executive leader of one of our nation's most powerful Bible Schools. His loyalty has been rewarded with a place of greater servanthood.

### For Group Discussion

1. How important have you found the character qualities of Psalm 101:5-7 to be, in choosing leaders?

2. Are there any other qualities you would add to that list of five?

3. Can you think of a time when you made the mistake of promoting someone who hadn't demonstrated loyalty? What were the results?

4. Do you agree with this statement about Korah—"The disloyal servant will never be the intercessor God needs, so he will not be promoted by God"?

5. Discuss the statement, "Tenure does not guarantee loyalty," and what it means for your team.

# CHAPTER 8

## *Loyalty And Love*

**L**oyalty has to do with love.[1] Where there is loyalty there is love. *Loyalty does not exist apart from love.*

The Bible says that love "bears all things, believes all things, hopes all things, endures all things" (1 Corinthians 13:7). Loyalty is a very intense form of love, so we might say, "Loyalty believes all things"—that is, it always believes the best in another. When rumors would seek to discredit another, loyalty has more faith in the person than the rumors. Loyalty believes in the sincerity of the other's motives, so that even when the facts would appear incriminating, loyalty still believes the heart intentions of the loved one are noble.

### *"Do You Love Me?"*

Knowing that love and loyalty are interconnected, the great, haunting question of all Scripture is Jesus' question to Peter, "'Do you love Me?'" (John 21:15). This becomes the foremost soul-searching question of all the ages. Jesus came to the man who had just denied Him three times and confronted him with the loyalty question. Jesus knew the Holy Spirit would come at Pentecost and seal Peter's loyalty; but for now, Jesus wanted Peter to search his heart.

The question echoes through the corridors of the centuries all the

---

[1] Jesus made a clear connection between love and loyalty. As we noted before, He said, "'No one can serve two masters; for either he will hate the one and love the other, or else he will be loyal to the one and despise the other. You cannot serve God and mammon'" (Matthew 6:24). The parallel construction of Jesus' argument puts the words "love" and "be loyal" together. Jesus was saying that to love a master and be loyal to a master are basically synonymous ideas.

way down to you and me: "Do you love Me?" There is no more important question to be answered, either now or at the foot of Christ's throne. It's the question of loyalty.

When Peter affirmed his love and loyalty for Christ, Jesus' reply was, "'Feed My sheep'" (John 21:17). Jesus was saying, "If you're really loyal to Me, you will express that loyalty by serving and feeding those that I love. Loyalty to Me means that you'll be willing to die for them, even as I died for them." This is why loyalty can have no element of self-preservation in it; it is willing to lay down its life.

### The Highest Form Of Love

Loyalty is not afraid to say, "I love you." Nor is it hesitant to demonstrate its love in concrete action. However, loyalty goes beyond love. Yes, it is an expression of love; but it's more than just love. Let me explain.

The Bible commands us to love others—we are to love our brothers and sisters in Christ fervently (1 Peter 1:22), we are to love sinners (Luke 15:2-4), and we are even to love our enemies (Matthew 5:44). We are commanded to love one another with a true *agapé* love, which is a selfless love that prefers others over oneself. We are never commanded, however, to be loyal to each other. Why not? Because *while love can be commanded, loyalty cannot*. Loyalty is an intense form of love that cannot be generated simply with determination or willpower.

*While we must love everyone, it is impossible to be loyal to everyone. We love all, but we're loyal to only a few.* Loyalty loves, but it goes a step beyond love. For example, I have many friends that I love dearly, but I have a loyalty to my wife and children that operates at a higher level. If I'm forced to prefer either a friend or my wife, loyalty to my wife will win out. Just as there are different degrees of love, there are differing intensities of loyalty.

Love is unconditional and universal; loyalty is selective. Love is directed toward all men, loyalty to a few.

*Loyalty is love to the second power.* It is *agapé* love squared. It is a form of love that is so noble, pure, honorable, and desirable that it cannot be commanded, demanded, expected, contrived, manufactured, or created. It is a gift of God. *When God gives it, there is loyalty; when God doesn't give it, no amount of energy can produce it.*

John wrote about "perfect love" (1 John 4:18). There is no doubt, when love has been made perfect within us, loyalty will shine from the heart in brilliance and purity.

The difference between love and loyalty is seen in the love that Ruth and Orpah had for their mother-in-law, Naomi. Orpah loved Naomi dearly and wept profusely when Naomi indicated that she was returning to her home town of Bethlehem. Orpah even indicated that she was going to accompany Naomi back to Bethlehem, saying, "'Surely we will return with you to your people'" (Ruth 1:10). Naomi, however, went into a long and convincing argument of why that was not in their best interests. Finally, Orpah acquiesced and kissed her mother-in-law good-bye. Orpah's love for Naomi was strong, beautiful, and beyond refute.

Ruth also loved her mother-in-law, Naomi. But her affection for Naomi went beyond love; it reached over into loyalty. Even after Naomi gave her most convincing arguments, Ruth refused to leave her side. Finally, Ruth gave what is commonly acknowledged as one of the most beautiful utterances of loyalty in the entire Bible:

> But Ruth said: "Entreat me not to leave you, or to turn back from following after you; for wherever you go, I will go; and wherever you lodge, I will lodge; your people shall be my people, and your God, my God. Where you die, I will die, and there will I be buried. The LORD do so to me, and more also, if anything but death parts you and me" (Ruth 1:16-17).

Naomi knew that she could never expect or request this kind of loyalty from her daughters-in-law. This was love, but it was such an intense display of love as to touch Naomi in the deepest places of the heart. Ever after, Naomi and Ruth were inseparable.

Jonathan had a similar affection for David. There can be no other explanation for it except that God sovereignly placed loyalty within the heart of Jonathan for David.

> Now when he had finished speaking to Saul, the soul of Jonathan was knit to the soul of David, and Jonathan loved him as his own soul...Then Jonathan and David made a covenant, because he loved him as his own soul. And Jonathan took off the robe that was on him and gave it to David, with his armor, even to his sword and his bow and his belt (1 Samuel 18:1,3-4).

Jonathan tied his heart to David because he heard the nobility of the man.

*Wherever there's a David, you'll probably find both an Absalom and a Jonathan.* Absalom just comes as part of the package for God's Davids. God uses Absalom's disloyalty to keep David broken and humble in the midst of promotion and great spiritual victories. And where there's a David there's a Jonathan. Jonathan was loyal to David even though he recognized that David would be the next king instead of himself. Jonathan's love was loyal and true. What a glorious thing it is when God gives to His Davids those Jonathans who will be loyal in spirit and who will love, even if it means that David's sphere will take precedence over their own.

Sometimes loyalty is violated, damaged, or ruined. However, even in instances when it has been shattered, love must still remain. *There is never sufficient cause to cease loving.* "Love never fails" (1 Corinthians 13:8). When David could no longer be loyal to Saul, he never failed to honor Saul with a godly love.

### For Group Discussion

1. Discuss your understanding of the relationship between loyalty and love.
2. *"Loyalty is love to the second power."* Do you agree? Have you ever seen this kind of love demonstrated?
3. Look at Ruth's words of loyalty to Naomi. How does this passage speak to the relationships within your group? Is there any sense in which you might be afraid to say the same words yourself? If so, why?
4. How is Song of Solomon 8:6 a graphic picture of loyalty to Christ and His loyalty to us? (View the verse as our speaking to Christ, as well as Christ's speaking the same words back to us.)

# CHAPTER 9

## *Our Loyalty To God Will Be Proven*

*I*f you stay with God long enough, eventually your loyalty to God will be tested. It took about three years during Jesus' earthly ministry, but finally everybody got offended at Jesus—the crowds, His family, His disciples, the religious leaders—everybody. It's but a matter of time. The offence is part of the test of loyalty. "Do you love Me?" God will test our loyalty in order to strengthen and purify our love.

God was wise to strengthen marriage with covenant vows because most couples end up getting offended at each other. After the honeymoon is over, spouses begin to discover characteristics in each other they didn't know existed. Without loyalty, most marriages would collapse. It's their loyalty to their covenant vows that carries couples through, until they come to celebrate each other's uniqueness.

The same thing happens in our covenant relationship with God. Things may start off on a great note. Then, as the years go by, God may allow something to happen to us that totally offends us. We begin to realize there are aspects of Jesus' personality that are different from what we thought. So He asks us, "Do you still love Me?" Loyalty will carry our hearts through the offence, until we come to know Christ in a deeper way than ever before. Sometimes, loyalty truly does get offended; but it always perseveres to the other side. By the time the test is over, we're more lovesick than ever!

### *Questioning God's Leadership Style*

The thing that proves our loyalty to God, in a word, is tribulation.

Loyalty is proven when God's goodness comes into question. Tribulation has a way of raising all the hidden questions of the heart. If there's anything within us that might doubt the goodness of God, tribulation will expose it. Pain has a way of cutting through all façades. It's when the path before us appears to be cruel that we discover our true convictions about God's character and kindness.

Loyalty to God, in the final analysis, comes down to whether or not we embrace His leadership style. God leads His family differently at times than we might expect. Scripture says it pleased the Father to crush (or bruise) His Son, Jesus Christ.[1] When God crushes you (a common element of His leadership style), will you still remain loyal to Him?

When He disciplines us, it's very tempting to begin to doubt the wisdom of how God is handling the affairs of our lives, and whether He's leading us in the right way and time. When we question His leadership style, we're sipping Lucifer's cup.

In the midst of the greatest pain, the loyal heart maintains that God is good. The greatest example of that truth is Jesus Himself. In His moment of greatest suffering, as He was about to exhale His last gasp of air on the cross, He offered His heart to God with these words of absolute trust and unwavering fidelity, "'Father, into Your hands I commit My spirit'" (Luke 23:46). Jesus was basically saying, "Even if You kill Me I'll still love You, because I know You. And I know You are good." No amount of apparent injustice could move Jesus' heart. His knowledge of the Father empowered Him to be loyal to the end.

God is still testing and proving the loyalty of His servants with the cross. He invites His servants to share in the sufferings of Christ, a suffering that proves the mettle of our loyalty. When loyalty is proven, God can entrust His chosen ones with greater spheres of responsibility.

Initially, when disciplined by God, our spirit will close up in a self-protecting mode, and we will very likely question the goodness of God. But like Job, we will begin a spiritual journey to find an open spirit to God in the midst of incredible pain. The key is in constantly giving Him our face, our heart, and our love. If we do, He will restore us to wholeheartedness. Job found an open spirit when he was finally able

---

[1] Isaiah 53:10.

to say, "Though He slay me, yet will I trust Him" (Job 13:15).

Will we be loyal to God, even in the midst of great distress? God uses the affairs of this life to settle this question in our souls before we step into glory. He wants to bring to glory many sons who have emerged from the crucible holding to the conviction that God is good and kind and faithful. God wants the loyalty issue resolved here on earth so that He doesn't have a repeat of the Lucifer incident all over again with mankind. God is in the business of raising up lovesick worshipers who are riveted by the wisdom of God's purposes and captured with admiration over the wonder of His decisions and judgments. These worshipers will cry out, "'All nations shall come and worship before You, for Your judgments have been manifested'" (Revelation 15: 4). God's leadership decisions (His judgments) evoke praise from the hearts of His loyal sons.

Loyal sons conclude, "I couldn't be in a better place, Lord, than in Your hands! The wisdom of the path You've chosen for my life is impeccable, flawless, and incapable of being improved upon."

### When We Can't Figure God Out

It will be glorious to be under God's perfect leadership in heaven. Even as all the people were pleased with all that King David did,[2] we will be pleased with all that the Son of David will do as He leads us. However, I think there will be times when we will not understand all of God's decisions on the front end. Some people seem to think heaven will be this place where we will finally understand and agree with all the legislation enacted. But God has never given us that assurance. The evidence would indicate that once we get to heaven, God will continue to make decisions that we will sometimes find baffling. To this very moment the angels in heaven continue to be perplexed by much of God's decision-making. (1 Peter 1:12 reveals that the angels are not included in all of God's strategies and so they gaze upon the earthly drama with keen curiosity to see how events will transpire.) God is eternally sovereign, and He will forever reserve the right to enforce decisions without fully explaining Himself in advance.

I'm suggesting you may have moments in eternity when you may think, "Wow! I would never have done what God is doing right now. I

---

[2] 2 Samuel 3:36.

55

wonder what He's up to!" When God doesn't do things your way, how will you respond? Will you trust Him in loyalty, or question Him? I believe eternity will continue to unfold decisions by the Godhead which will baffle and perplex us, cause us to be intrigued, and draw us to gaze with fresh fascination at the magnificence of God's wisdom and ways. By the time each story is finished, we will stand in awe at the goodness and grace of our God.

The fact that a third of heaven's angels turned away from God would support the premise that heaven is not a place where all opinions are magically made to be identical. (Even Jesus had to defer to the Father's will—which He did with dignity because He was a loyal Son—revealing that differences of will sometimes occur even within the Godhead.) But heaven is a place where, because of the deep affections of our hearts for the beautiful Son of God, we will all come into one judgment.[3] We will agree with God's judgments simply because He is the one saying this is the way it needs to be.

God uses this age to prepare us for the next by seeing whether we will follow the ministries that He gives to the body in this age. He has gifted us with apostles, prophets, evangelists, pastors, and teachers,[4] who are called of God to bring leadership to the body. Sometimes we find ourselves questioning or even disagreeing with decisions they make. Our loyalty to these ministries here on earth is just a trial run for the real thing. Our responses now prepare us for the eternal city where loyalty's value cannot be overstated.

Twelve years ago (as of this writing), I collided with the God who fries your theological circuits. Something happened to me for which I didn't have a scriptural grid. God allowed me to suffer a debilitating vocal injury that happened in the context of pouring my life out in labor for Him. I got offended at God. At times, if I were honest, I would even have to admit I was mad at God. "How could You allow this to happen to me? Did You do this? And if You did, who are You anyway?" I found myself questioning whether I even knew this God that I was serving.

I have always sought to be a worshiper at heart, and now I found my worship being challenged at its foundations. Could I look into His eyes and say, "I still love You"? My loyalty to God has been challenged at the core of my being, but as I have persevered through the offence

[3] 1 Corinthians 1:10.
[4] Ephesians 4:11-12.

and given Him my love, I can testify that my loyalty to Him is stronger than ever.

I believe that one reason God is proving the loyalty of His people in this hour is because the day is coming, not long from now, when God will pour out His judgments on the earth, and men will gnash their teeth in rage against God.[5] In that day, those whose loyalty to God has been proven—and has come through purified—will be able to help others interpret God's judgments as the necessary measures of a merciful and lovesick God to produce the greatest harvest of souls possible before the end of the age. This is why judgment begins at the house of God, with God's people (1 Peter 4:17). When we pass through judgment, we will be constrained to find a way to interpret our pain levels in the light of God's goodness. That understanding, articulated clearly, will serve unbelievers who are questioning the goodness of God in the day of His wrath. In that hour, only the loyal will be able to represent God's heart accurately to others.

Loyalty to God empowers us to come through the hour of testing to a place where we know Him better, are fascinated by His personality, are more lovesick than ever, and even more loyal in our hearts. But for those who are not loyal, the crucible can cause them to crash and burn. When God reveals Himself to be different than we expected, loyalty is the seal on the heart[6] that carries us through the turbulence and perplexity until we see the unfolding of God's purposes.

In an ironic contrast to all of that, another way God proves our loyalty is through blessing. The history of the nation of Israel reveals a tendency in all of us. When God began to bless and prosper them, that was the time they were most easily turned away from their loyalty to God. This is seen so clearly in King Solomon's life. Early in his reign, Solomon called the nation to loyalty: "'Let your heart therefore be loyal to the LORD our God, to walk in His statutes and keep His commandments, as at this day'" (1 Kings 8:61). But then God began to prosper Solomon mightily, and slowly his heart began to turn. It's sad but true—he turned away from his loyalty to God in his old age. "For it was so, when Solomon was old, that his wives turned his heart after other gods; and his heart was not loyal to the LORD his God, as

---

[5] Revelation 16:11.
[6] See Song of Solomon 8:6.

was the heart of his father David" (1 Kings 11:4). Success has such an insidious way of eroding our loyalty to God that it even found its mark with a man as wise and anointed as Solomon.

So whether it's a time of success or distress, prepare your heart: Your loyalty will be tested.

### How Jacob's Loyalty Was Proven

Nothing seems to test loyalty like a good, long wait. David learned something about that when he hesitated, at the end of his reign, to install Solomon as king. He hesitated because he saw something lacking in Solomon. He knew what God had done in his own life by causing him to be chased down by Saul for his life, living in caves, forests, wildernesses, and strongholds. It was a fiery crucible, and it prepared David for the challenges of success. But Solomon had no such crucible to help prepare him for the success he was inheriting. David hesitated, not sure Solomon could handle the success without self-destructing. It turns out his fears were well founded. But while David delayed, the wait tested the loyalties of everyone in his court. The long wait ended up revealing disloyalty in the hearts of his commander (Joab), his priest (Abiathar), and his son (Adonijah).[7] All three of them turned in disloyalty against David and tried to overthrow him. Had David not waited so long to install Solomon, their disloyalties would have never manifested.

Similarly, the greatest test of faith and loyalty is when we must wait on God for a long time. I want to use Jacob as our example here. Jacob was a man who demonstrated his loyalty to God by waiting on Him. One of the compelling aspects of Jacob's life was how often he was required to wait on God for the salvation of the Lord. Here's a rough outline of Jacob's life—consider the lengthy seasons of waiting he endured.

- Wait 35 years, then God does something.[8]
- Wait 40 more years, then God does something else.[9]
- Wait 20 more years, then God does something else.[10]

[7] 1 Kings 1:5-53.
[8] Genesis 25:29-34.
[9] Genesis 28:10-22.
[10] Genesis 32:22-32.

- Wait 13 more years, then God does something else.[11]
- Wait 22 more years, then God reveals His mighty salvation (at age 130).[12]
- Enjoy 17 years of God's abundance (before dying at age 147).[13]

Jacob was a man who had come into covenant with God after a divine encounter. He was on his way to Padam Aram, had stopped in Bethel for an overnight sleep, and was visited by God in a dream. God was the first one to speak:

> And behold, the LORD stood above it and said: "I am the LORD God of Abraham your father and the God of Isaac; the land on which you lie I will give to you and your descendants. Also your descendants shall be as the dust of the earth; you shall spread abroad to the west and the east, to the north and the south; and in you and in your seed all the families of the earth shall be blessed. Behold, I am with you and will keep you wherever you go, and will bring you back to this land; for I will not leave you until I have done what I have spoken to you" (Genesis 28:13-15).

Jacob was so overwhelmed by God's promises of blessing that he expressed his desire to reciprocate:

> Then Jacob made a vow, saying, "If God will be with me, and keep me in this way that I am going, and give me bread to eat and clothing to put on, so that I come back to my father's house in peace, then the LORD shall be my God. And this stone which I have set as a pillar shall be God's house, and of all that You give me I will surely give a tenth to You" (Genesis 28:20).

Jacob said, "God, if You'll do such and such, then I'll do such and such." And God accepted the challenge. Twenty years later, Jacob returned to his homeland, by which time God had met all the conditions of the covenant. So the Lord came to Jacob to finalize the covenant.[14] Jacob wrestled with a Man all night, who put his hip out

---

[11] Genesis 37:31-36.
[12] Genesis 46:29.
[13] Genesis 47:28.
[14] See Genesis 32:22-32.

of socket and changed his name to Israel. Jacob called the place Peniel ("Face of God"), for he saw God face to face and lived. God was basically saying, "Jacob, I kept my part of the deal. You've returned to your homeland in peace. Now, will you be true to your side of the deal? Will I now be your God? Will you now be loyal to Me?" Jacob said, "Yes"; he sealed the covenant with God, and fully gave his loyalty to God.

However, Jacob's fidelity was only beginning to be tested. God was about to take Jacob through the greatest tests of his life. It all began when God removed his favorite son, Joseph, from his life. Jacob thought he was dead, but Joseph was a slave in Egypt. It would be 22 years before they would be reunited.

Then, toward the end of the 22-year wait, a famine struck the land with such fury that many nations were without food. Like other foreigners, Jacob's family went to Egypt to get food. But the man in Egypt imprisoned Simeon, and he demanded that the brothers return only if they had Benjamin with them.

Jacob was in anguish. He had lost Joseph, now he had lost Simeon, and the man wanted Benjamin! "Never!" he cried. "Over my dead body will the man have Benjamin!"

"It just may be over your dead body," the sons replied, "Because this famine has a terrible grip on the land, and we're all starving to death. If you don't let Benjamin return with us, we're all going to die!"

Not only had Jacob lost two of his sons, but it seemed like God Himself was against him, causing this famine to squeeze the very life out of their souls (for Jacob knew that God is sovereign over the weather). He didn't want to relinquish Benjamin, but there seemed to be no options. Finally Jacob uttered a great visceral cry, "'Everything is against me!'"[15]

Jacob was 130 years old; he had served God for many years; but instead of reaping the blessings of covenant, everything was being stripped away from him. He didn't understand the silence of God, nor why heaven seemed to be crushing him.

But here's the great shining reality in the midst of the story: Jacob never broke his loyalty to God! Even at the cost of losing Benjamin, he

---

[15] Genesis 42:36, NIV.

was resolved to remain loyal to his covenant with God. It's in the presence of disappointment that loyalty sparkles its diamond-like beauty, for loyalty continues to love even in the face of disappointment.

And how God honored Jacob for it! Within approximately three weeks' time, everything turned for Jacob, and he suddenly beheld the mighty salvation of God. He was transported to Egypt in the most modern limo of the day; he was reunited with all his sons; he blessed Pharaoh; he saw his entire family established in prosperity; he was able to bless all his sons before his death; and he received the funeral of a king. He went out in style!

While blessing his sons at the end of his life, Jacob declared, "'I have waited for your salvation, O LORD!'" (Genesis 49:18). No one who knows Jacob's story could argue with that statement. If anyone had waited for God, over and over, it was Jacob. His loyalty to God was proven again and again. And now we acknowledge him as one of the great fathers of our faith. In fact, we worship "the God of Jacob." His loyalty was proven through the wait, and now he is honored with an everlasting posterity like the stars of the heavens.

"Happy is he who has the God of Jacob for his help" (Psalm 146: 5). Happy is he who is loyal to God through the wait, for God will help and visit him.

### *For Group Discussion*

1.  Has your loyalty to Christ ever been tested? Explain.
2.  Do you know what it's like for your spirit to close in the wake of God's disciplines? If so, how was your spirit restored to openness before God?
3.  Consider how God leads differently from how we sometimes expect. How will we process this aspect of God's personality in the age to come? Do you agree with the author that our loyalty to God may be tested in the age to come when God makes decisions we don't fully understand?
4.  Some people hold little respect for Jacob. The author, in contrast, paints Jacob as a man of spiritual greatness who demonstrated great loyalty to God. How do you see Jacob?
5.  Are you waiting on God right now for a specific breakthrough? Is the wait proving your loyalty?

# PART TWO

# Loyalty To God's Davids

When our loyalty to God is tested and our love purified, giving our hearts in loyalty to God's leaders becomes the most natural and reasonable thing to do. We can know our loyalty to God is true when it is expressed through loyalty to others in the body of Christ.

# CHAPTER 10

# *Taking On The Cultural Giants*

*L*oyalty to God finds its natural expression in loyalty to people. The one leads directly into the other. Someone who is loyal to God will also desire to be loyal to God's Davids. Our discussion, therefore, naturally causes us to turn and consider our loyalty to our fellow man.

As long as we say we should be loyal to God, no one has a problem with that. The problem comes when we take it to the next level and say we should be loyal to God's Davids. When we start talking about loyalty to another human being, the issues become complicated.

Calling people to loyalty runs in the face of some cultural values that have been commonly accepted by Americans. There are some "giants" in the land of loyalty, and if our call to loyalty is to be effective we must at least be aware of these potential hindrances.

### Sociological Giants

Loyalty is not totally un-American. There are some respects, in fact, in which Americans are intensely loyal. Most fans will root for their favorite professional sports team even if they are at the bottom of the league. Inner city street gangs are held together by loyalty. Many companies have been able to cultivate enduring sales success for their products by securing "brand loyalty." Labor unions function on the premise of loyalty. Since the bombing of New York City's Twin Towers on 9-11-01, Americans have bonded together in more national solidarity than our nation has seen for several decades. Perhaps it's more than happenstance that this book is being written during a sociological upswing of loyalty.

There are, however, biases against loyalty that still exist in our culture and that require our attention. Some biases are found among the older segment of our population who lived through the revolutionary atmosphere of the 1960's. We have had times in our recent history when it has been culturally acceptable to be anti-establishment or anti-government.

School children will insult our American President and then be assured by their teachers that this freedom of speech is their right. Those who dishonor the fathers and leaders of our nation are sometimes lauded as independent thinkers. We'll even wink at flag-burning. We tolerate forms of civil disobedience that undermine the very values that strengthen society's social fabric (I do not mean that all forms of civil disobedience fall into this negative category).

When it comes to movies, novels, and literature, many of the stories that entertain us are built around loyalty. However, there are others that undermine it. *One of the great American values is "loyalty to self," a value which often takes precedence ethically over loyalty to others.* This brand of self-loyalty, rooted in self-love, militates against biblical loyalty.

In the workplace, loyalty faces another set of challenges. Most workers are repulsed by those who will sidle up to the boss in order to gain his or her favor. We hated "the teacher's pet" in school, and now on the job we often despise those who will swallow their personal convictions or compromise their souls in order to climb the corporate ladder. While loyalty may be honored by the boss, it's likely to be punished by other employees. Thus, it is sometimes perceived as a quality that incurs trouble, conflict, and reproach.

*The general effect of these biases is that the value of loyalty in society is sometimes eroded.*

Loyalty is highly important to kings and to kingdoms, even moreso than to democracies or republics. Kings reward loyalty and punish disloyalty; democracies tolerate disloyalty and don't always esteem loyalty. So while it may not always be appreciated in a republic like America, it is to be highly valued in the Kingdom of God.

### Ecclesiastical Giants

In addition to battling these "cultural giants" of modern society, there are also dynamics at work in the church world that have contributed to the deterioration of loyalty among Christians. For example, there are many believers who were loyal in the past to their church leaders but became deeply hurt in the process. Perhaps a leader became filled with a sense of self-importance, or maybe fell into moral compromise, or became controlling and manipulative in his or her leadership style. I have friends who served in ministries where the leader held loyalty as a measuring rod over their heads, demanding their loyalties if they were to stay on the ministry team. Loyalty has become a painful word to these folks.

In the wake of the anti-establishment movement of the 1960's, the pendulum began to swing the other way. The Jesus Movement saw an influx into the church of believers who, rejecting the values of the hippie movement and Woodstock and Berkeley, were looking for oversight and accountability. Consequently, there came a call for submission to authority and for covenantal relationships. This emphasis was born of the Spirit and pervaded many streams and denominations across the body of Christ. God was breathing upon this emphasis, but the pendulum continued to swing, and some groups strayed into excessive authority structures.

Some leaders exerted excessive control over their members, even to the point of telling them where to live and what to buy. The land became strewn with spiritual casualties—people who lost their trust in all spiritual authority and who struggled to find a functional way to relate to the body of Christ. Like many pastors in the 1980's and 1990's, I found myself faced with the challenge of ministering to many people who looked like the "burnt stones" of the book of Nehemiah—saints who were charred and avoided being cemented into places of commitment in the wall. Many of them were so tender that any hint of desiring loyalty would have sent them scurrying away.

I know of churches who had Covenant Commitments comprised of seven or more pages of written material, which adherents signed, and copies were kept on file by the church leaders. It was considered a noble thing to enter into sworn covenant with a given group of believers, presumably for life (all things being equal). The problems began when people chose to move on. Instead of being released joyfully, they were called covenant breakers and often disbarred from fellowshiping with other members. For some, loyalty became a four-letter word.

We still suffer fallout today. Sometimes a believer who has become skeptical or cynical toward authority will see another member giving his heart in loyalty to a leader. Thinking they're doing a favor, the skeptical member will warn the innocent member, infecting the other member with their own offence. Many believers today have unresolved baggage regarding this topic, and when they spread the yeast of their own hurt to those with simplicity of heart, it undermines the health of the body. A root of bitterness can quickly defile others in the body of Christ, but since a root grows below the surface, it can operate for quite a while before it is noticed by those who could help. *Unfortunately, disloyalty is usually more contagious than loyalty.*

The fact is, some leaders still abuse loyalty. Therefore, I do not mean for this book to be interpreted as defending controlling, manipulative leadership styles. However, I will not be silent—as others may have been—simply because some leadership styles are excessive. Rather, I will sound the call to loyalty, believing the Holy Spirit will help us discern how to apply these principles in each individual situation.

And I'm encouraged by something that is stirring in the land. Today's generation values loyalty more than their forefathers. They *want* to give their hearts to the fathers and mothers. Young people today value loyalty despite the sociological and ecclesiological influences to the contrary, a development that I believe is the direct work of God as He is preparing the hearts of a generation for His return.

### Loyalty Is Often Misinterpreted

Be prepared: If you are loyal to David, you will quite likely be misunderstood. (Remember—David is representative of godly leaders deserving our loyalty. The Bible commended those who were loyal to David, and God still calls us to be loyal to His Davids today—those leaders who have a heart after God and a jealousy for the fame of Christ's name in the earth. Your David may be male or female, but God has placed that leader in your life and now will honor you as you honor him or her.)

Loyalty is easily misread or misconstrued. For example, a loyal employee ends up being called a "company man." Or a loyal elder or deacon is called a "yes man." People will accuse a certain pastor of surrounding himself with "yes men." In some cases that may be true. But is it possible that some pastors have enough wisdom to surround themselves with loyal leaders?

*One difference between a yes man and a loyal man is this: A yes man finds his identity through his association with the leader, so he will consciously or subconsciously modify his words and behavior to protect his position before the leader. A loyal man, in contrast, will find his identity in who he is before the throne of God, which gives him the freedom to love his leader unconditionally—but also gives him the freedom to give the leader feedback from a heart of sincerity, honesty, openness, and wisdom.* Loyal men and women are not afraid to speak the truth in love because they are more concerned about serving the leader than protecting their own status with the leader.

I know a pastor who had a woman in his congregation who was a tremendous servant. She served in his leadership team as an invaluable asset, completing all assigned tasks with cheerfulness and diligence. The pastor was so thankful to God for her support and help in the work of the Lord.

There happened to be someone else on the leadership team, however, who misunderstood her loyalty. This other sister thought her friend was being influenced by the pastor's charisma and strong personality. Instead of perceiving the sister's loyalty, she thought the sister was motivated by a personal need to win the pastor's approval.

Thinking she was doing the right thing, she went to the sister and basically said, "It seems to me that you're motivated more by a desire to please a man than to please God." The sister was taken aback. What had she done to give that impression?

From that time on, that sister never again served her pastor with the same freedom. She drew back, fearful of how she was being perceived by others. A fountain of servanthood was quenched, and in its place came reservation, hesitancy, and aloofness. She didn't know how to handle the accusation of bowing to the fear of man. As a result, the kingdom suffered loss. Her loyalty was violated, and she was never again able to recover it to the same degree.

Experiences like this show that when loyalty is not properly understood and appreciated, it can be easily misinterpreted. We must stand against the cultural enemies that would cause us to view loyalty through a skewed lens. The stakes are enormous. We cry for the restoration of David's tabernacle (Amos 9:11), but how can we have the restoration of David's tabernacle without the loyalty that surrounded David? I'm convinced that loyalty is a seriously overlooked ingredient that must be recovered for the church to enter into her fullness in the last hour.

### *For Group Discussion*

1.  What biases have you noticed in society that would seem to undermine loyalty? Have you seen other elements in the culture that would affirm loyalty as a desirable quality?

2.  Have you known anyone in the church who has been a spiritual casualty from loyalty gone awry? How has it affected their fruitfulness in the Kingdom? How can we repair the damage that's been done?

3.  Would you agree that today's generation is desiring loyal relationships perhaps even more than the previous generation?

4.  Has your loyalty ever been misinterpreted?

# CHAPTER 11

## *Caricatures Of Loyalty*

O ne reason loyalty has been maligned in the church is that many believers have a distorted concept of its true beauty. Maybe they've seen people who were loyal to a fault. Or maybe they were under a leader who called for loyalty, but its meaning was warped. As a result, when some people think of loyalty, they envision something that is actually a distorted and frightening aberration of the genuine.

Before we continue, therefore, we need to dismantle some wrong ideas. I want to be clear about what I *don't* mean to be saying. Briefly, here are three things loyalty is not.

### Loyalty Is Not Naïve

*First, loyalty is not naïve about a leader's weaknesses.* It realizes that the leader is but flesh. It has no delusions of serving under a Superman or Superwoman. Loyalty is not a romantic unrealism, nor must it be enamored with the leader.

Loyalty does not mean we exalt a leader above measure. If we exalt David above measure, God has to take measures to keep David humble. People were tempted to exalt Paul above measure because of his incredible revelations, and so God gave Paul a thorn in his flesh (a physical affliction that was visible to others) to get him back down to size in the eyes of people.[1] Loyalty is not the putting of a leader on a pedestal, but it is the honoring of a leader as the appointed pacesetter, the "set man" or "set woman," a blessing from God given to serve the church.

[1] See 2 Corinthians 12.

To be loyal does not mean we put our trust in man. We are counseled, "Do not put your trust in princes, nor in a son of man, in whom there is no help. His spirit departs, he returns to his earth; in that very day his plans perish" (Psalm 146:3-4). Those who put their trust in a person will always be disappointed. *Be loyal to David, but trust in God alone.*

Loyalty is not in denial of a leader's humanity, nor is it merely the domain of the gullible who can't perceive a leader's shortcomings. Rather, it's the adornment of those who are loyal despite a leader's weaknesses. *Loyalty flourishes best when the son is fully aware of the father's weak areas.*

Neither is loyalty naïve about a father's failures toward other sons. Every leader has a learning curve; virtually every father has failures in his past regarding how he handled his sons. *Loyalty realizes that David doesn't father every son perfectly.* If we were to be loyal only to those fathers who handled us perfectly, there would be very little loyalty in the land today.

*Loyalty may even realize that some sons have left the father in the past with a valid grievance.* Loyalty sometimes watches other sons come and go. They may even leave muttering things under their breath like, "he's controlling," or "she's unappreciative," or "he's a taskmaster," or "she doesn't deliver what she promises," or "he doesn't know how to release areas of ministry," or "he doesn't know how to pastor people's gifts."

Sometimes David blew it. People forsook David for valid reasons. But at the end of the day, the all-important question was, are you with Absalom or David? Because God likes David, issues and all, and He fights for him. *Whether the grievances are partly valid or invalid, the loyal son who chooses to stay with David does so, not because he's unsympathetic to the other sons, but because he refuses to pick up their offence.* He realizes that David has made his mistakes, but he still chooses to love and to stay at David's side. The loyal son has decided he wants to be on the team of the man with the promises, foibles and all.

*A true son realizes that every strength has its corresponding weakness, so the father's strengths and giftings of necessity must have their attending liabilities.* The son is drawn to the father because of the God-deposit in his life, but then in loyalty he does his best to cover the accompanying weaknesses. Far from being naïve about the leader's shortcomings, the loyal person—through proximity—is perhaps more aware of them than anyone else.

### Loyalty Is Not Unqualified Allegiance

Paul clearly declared that loyalty to Christ is unqualified, but loyalty to God's leaders is in a lesser, conditional category.[2]

Loyalty doesn't get a lobotomy. It is not mindless adherence. If the leader says to you, "Here, drink this vial," and you drink it and fall over dead, that's not loyalty; that's stupidity.

Some might look at excessive expressions of loyalty and call it "blind loyalty," but if it's blind it's not loyalty. Because *loyalty is not blind*. Nor does it give itself without exercising discernment.

Loyalty thinks for itself. And yet, some brands of loyalty do not allow for independent thinking. There is a tension here that affects various groups, such as the military. So let's look a bit at the military.

Loyalty is highly valued by the military and is extolled during the training season. It keeps a battalion together, empowering them as a group to accomplish greater exploits than if they were alone and separated. Some of the greatest loyalty stories told are to be found in the annals of war. For example, perhaps you've heard of the soldier who stepped forward into enemy fire in order to rescue his wounded comrade. Nations will award with medals of honor their heroes who, in the face of great odds and terrifying danger, were loyal to their fellow soldiers. These heroic kinds of stories move every one of our hearts.

*While implicit obedience is demanded in the military, there is a greater dimension of loyalty that troops will hold for a superior who has demonstrated his willingness to sacrifice personally for the sake of his men.* The greatest officers are those who not only command obedience because of positional authority, but who inspire an affectionate allegiance from their troops because they have demonstrated a selfless interest in their welfare and destiny.

But some military officers demand obedience on the merit of their superior position alone. Troops may give that kind of leader their absolute obedience, but they won't give him their loyalty. A gruff military

[2] 1 Corinthians 1:12-13.

officer might growl, "Don't think, don't question, just obey." We are not subscribing to this brand of loyalty, however. *Loyalty in the Kingdom is not unquestioning obedience to a leader but is full of wisdom and discretion.*

Circumstances may occasionally surface in which one must disobey earthly leaders in order to remain obedient to God. Others may regard us as disloyal in such cases, but *our loyalty to God supercedes all loyalties to man.*

Some ministries operate like a mini-military. Loyalty is defined as unquestioning submission to leadership. While this mentality may be present in some brigades, it is not the way of the Kingdom.

Loyalty does not enter into a blood covenant with a group of believers, saying, "I am yours, no matter what." It must be distinguished from cultish forms of allegiance. Loyalty has its head screwed on straight. It says, "I'm with you—as long as Jesus is your first pursuit, and you don't get weird on us."

David doesn't need numb, unthinking followers. Rather, he needs loyal helpers who will contribute the best of their mental energies to the cause.

As a small aside, a controversial book has been released at the time of this writing, entitled, *The Price Of Loyalty.* The author, Pulitzer Prize-winning Ron Suskind, tells the story of Paul O'Neill's 23 months of service as Treasury Secretary under President George W. Bush. The book is not primarily about loyalty but about O'Neill's perspective on the inner workings of Bush's administration. I mention the book here because it's an example, in my opinion, of a man who believed our premise, "loyalty is not unqualified allegiance," but then took it to an excess.

The two-year working relationship between O'Neill and President Bush was not easy, almost from the start. One reason for that, according to Suskind, was that Bush demanded "loyalty to an individual, no matter what."[3] Cheney gave this kind of loyalty to Bush, which is why he has been trusted so implicitly by the President.[4] O'Neill was different.

O'Neill believed that "real loyalty...is loyalty based on inquiry, and

[3] The Price Of Loyalty, Ron Suskind, New York: Simon & Schuster, 2004, p. 326.
[4] Ibid., p. 48.

telling someone what you really think and feel—your best estimation of truth instead of what they want to hear."[5] Suskind suggests it was O'Neill's loyalty to inquiry and truth, rather than to the President, that eventually prompted Bush to ask for O'Neill's resignation.

After reading the book, it's my conviction that O'Neill never did find loyalty to Bush (that's an observation, not a criticism), which doubtless was a primary factor in his eventually being fired. While I do not fully subscribe to O'Neill's understanding of loyalty, I do agree that it is *not* mindless adherence. O'Neill found himself in the unenviable dilemma of not being able to be loyal to his leader because to do so would have required him to disregard the factual information he had gleaned. O'Neill published his criticisms of Bush's leadership style for the purpose of truth-telling.[6] However, in so doing, he stepped off the ground of neutrality onto the soil of disloyalty to President Bush, a decision that I consider regrettable.

### Loyalty Is Not Silent Acquiescence

Some models of church structure have the perspective that one should never question those who are over them in the Lord. I do not embrace this view of spiritual authority because it never produces true loyalty; rather, it produces clones, drones, and "yes men."

I've known of leaders who have not allowed their followers to question their decisions. If you disagreed you were labeled disloyal. For them, loyalty meant quiet agreement. *That's not loyalty, that's control borne out of insecurity.*

If a leader wants loyalty among his followers, one of the best things he can do is cultivate an atmosphere of openness to encourage feedback. If he is defensive every time a contrary opinion is expressed, he will lose others' loyalty. Friends work through differences of opinion in the same way that iron sharpens iron.[7] *Feedback happens best in the context of loyal friendships.* We're not talking about two people who just go at it and slay one another with their tongues. We're talking about two friends who, in the context of a loyal relationship, love each other enough to speak the truth and reflect necessary feedback to one another.

[5] Ibid., p. 326.
[6] Ibid., p. 328.
[7] Proverbs 27:17.

A loyal relationship not only *allows* the son to vocalize his concerns to the father, it *invites* that kind of honest interchange. A son needs to learn the art of appealing to others in the body of Christ.[8] Healthy structures allow the sons to appeal to the fathers in a safe environment of trusting exchange. Wise fathers want to train their sons in the art of loving confrontation and appeal.[9] Furthermore, wise fathers greatly value the perspectives of their sons, for they know the sons will help them serve more effectively. A loyal son will not withhold a perspective that would truly serve or save the father.

"Faithful are the wounds of a friend" (Proverbs 27:6). A friend, because he is loyal, is willing to confront—as painful as confrontation sometimes can be.

Loyalty disagrees, and even confronts. But loyalty is always very careful about *how* and *where* it disagrees.

*How* does loyalty disagree? Loyalty expresses itself in tenderness and love. *You can say anything you want to me; but if you're loyal to me, you'll say it gently in a way that helps me.* If you're loyal, you won't spew venom all over me, or blow me away with your gun. The disagreement may be intense, but it should not be caustic or hurtful. You'll be careful how you say it, believing the best in me.

*Where* does loyalty disagree? *Loyalty disagrees behind closed doors.* t doesn't express its dissent out in the midst of the rank and file. Loyalty will be honest and will work out the kinks behind closed doors. Then, when we come out into the mix of other people, we cover each other with a united front of agreement.

I remember one time when I learned how *not* to confront a spiritual father. I was young, with a lot of zeal, and I really wanted to be heard. However, because of the nature of my relationship to this particular leader, I went into the meeting already expecting that I wouldn't be heard. Instead of just stating my case and expressing my heart, I leaned into my argument with a little bit of extra energy, thinking that perhaps some additional arguments would help to tip the balance in my favor. The strength of my presentation worked against me, however, and basically invalidated what I was trying to communicate. Instead of being dismissed on the merit of my argument, I was dismissed because

[8] See Philemon 1:10.
[9] See 1 Timothy 5:1.

of the spirit in which I delivered my perspective. What's more, I got a rebuke for my trouble! So the lesson learned was, approach fathers in gentleness and good faith, believing the best, and expecting them to receive you.

### For Group Discussion

1.  When you see another aspect of your leader's weaknesses, does it shake your loyalty, or make it stronger?

2.  We have said in this chapter that loyalty is conditional. But how can we guard against people feeling justified in moving from one loyalty to another in serial fashion?

3.  How have you chosen to work out disagreements on your team? When is it right to speak up? And when is it right to be silent and go with the group?

4.  Have you ever felt intimidated to express your opinion to your leader?

# CHAPTER 12

## *Personal Versus Institutional Loyalty*

*L*oyalty is almost always to a person. Loyalty usually forms in the heart when we've been joined to someone whom we believe to have the heart of David.

*Whenever we see loyalty manifest in the Bible, it is always directed to a person—either to God, or to a human being.* Jonathan was loyal to David; Ruth to Naomi; Elisha to Elijah; the disciples to Jesus; Timothy and Titus to Paul. And the list goes on.

Conversely, disloyalty is almost always to a person. Disloyalty is often the violating of a bond of trust with one of God's Davids. It's the dishonoring of a relationship with a father in the faith. *When people are disloyal to David, usually it's because they're loyal either to Absalom or to themselves.*

A friend told me how he was losing his ability to receive from his pastor. He was struggling over an issue and found that his pastor's sermons were no longer feeding him. Instead, he was finding himself critical of everything coming out of the pastor's mouth, or how it was delivered. Then the Lord convicted his heart, and he repented sincerely before the Lord for his pride and judgmental spirit. The very next Sunday, his pastor's sermon was loaded with revelation and heart-impacting truth! When, through repentance, my friend had returned to loyalty, his heart had been opened, and he was again able to receive from his pastor.

Loyalty, directed properly to the David whom God has put in our lives, is such a powerful thing—little wonder the enemy targets it.

### *Personal Versus Institutional Loyalty*

*Loyalty seems to sustain best when it is directed toward an individual rather than an institution.* For example, when people decide to be loyal to the church of Jesus Christ, they often become disenchanted through disappointment and sometimes even make inner vows never to return to the church. In contrast, when people are loyal to the person of Christ Jesus, their love for Christ will often sustain them through the disappointments of life within the church's institutions.

Someone might say, "I'm loyal to my company," but a bad boss can destroy that quickly. Someone else might say, "I'm loyal to my church," but an unhappy confrontation with a pastor or leader can terminate that kind of loyalty. Another might say, "I'm loyal to my denomination." Perhaps you feel loyal to your denomination, but what will you do if they pass a bylaw that violates your convictions and conscience? I'm not suggesting that loyalty to an institution is bad or wrong; I'm simply saying that it is not necessarily enduring in the face of negative circumstances.

Organizations have a long history of disappointing loyalties. Most people who feel loyal to an organization are actually loyal to a leader or leaders who are in place at the time. When a David is at the helm of an institution, he will tend to draw those who want to give their loyalties to his leadership.

Institutional loyalty can be noble in its own right, but it can also be unwise. Some have lost their edge spiritually because they've chosen to remain with an institution when the blessing of God has lifted. What is the value of institutional loyalty if we lose our way spiritually as a result?

Lest someone think me to be against denominations, let me explain that I hold ministry credentials with an ordaining fellowship of ministers, and am still loyal to that organization after many years. However, I do not see that loyalty being as strong as that which I hold to individuals within that organization. It is commendable to be loyal to an institution in order to be a lifegiving contributor to the ministry and vision of the whole—even if our contribution is not completely understood or appreciated. We will have no voice to the great spiritual institutions of the earth without loyalty that endures.

The purpose of joining ourselves to an institution is so that through the network of relationships we develop, we can mutually serve, strengthen, and challenge each other's personal walk with God and sharpen the effectiveness of each other's ministry. To the degree the institution is effectively serving that goal is the degree to which we should be loyal to the institution.

Institutions are usually birthed out of the impact of a visionary leader who lost everything for the sake of the Gospel. However, as the years roll by, institutions inevitably default to a mode of self-preservation. *Mechanisms of self-preservation are Saulish in nature and are counter-productive to cultivating healthy loyalty.*

Our motive in being loyal to an institution can sometimes be based upon an inner desire to be promoted in the system. The best way to the top in institutions is to be loyal to the person or persons over you. It is assumed that if someone has been loyal in the system long enough, he or she now deserves a place of promotion. If the promotion is withheld, the person who has labored for years in the system sometimes turns in anger upon the very system he has served and devours his brothers and sisters with his words[1]. *Loyalty that is looking for repayment is not true loyalty.*

*Another kind of false loyalty occurs when a son is loyal to a father because he feels he owes the father something for what the father has done for him.* Once the son has paid the debt, he'll maintain his loyalty only if the father does him yet another favor. Loyalty based on favors cannot be maintained.

Institutional loyalty is often based upon the unspoken assumption, "You scratch my back, I'll scratch yours." The only way to get promoted in this kind of system is to stay in the system—even if it's not God's will for you to be there.

Loyalty to David, in contrast, is a joining of hearts, even if it means personal diminishment. The focus is upon doing the will of God in the now.

*Loyalty means that we help each other obey God today.* David doesn't say, "If you're loyal to me, eventually it will earn you a position in the system." Rather, David says, "If God has joined your heart to mine for this season, let's labor together for the advance of the Kingdom." He celebrates the times of co-laboring together, but then is also willing to release you to the will of God if He is calling you to another place.

[1] See Galatians 5:15.

Sometimes the most loyal thing you can do is leave. Because if God is calling you to move on, but you're staying so you can work your way up in the system, then you become a Jonah—someone who is with us outside the will of God. If God is calling you to another place, please do us a favor and let us help you get to where you need to go.

If we are inordinately committed to staying together against God's will, God will use pressure to move us out. This is what He did in the New Testament. In Acts 1:8 He called them to move out into Samaria; but when they didn't, He brought the pressure of Acts 8:1 to get them there. When God finally has to use relational pressure to send us forth into the harvest, it can come at the pricetag of many wounded relationships and hurt people. How much better when we see loyalty as a firm commitment to helping each other stay in the will of God, rather than trying to keep everyone huddled together within a given system.

In our brokenness, we want job security (within ministry systems or institutions) that assures us a secure future and no longer requires that we depend upon God to keep our calling and ministry alive. So, to provide that security, we formulate covenants with one another that appear to be founded in loyalty. But this is not true security. The place of real security is found when we place our "Isaac" (our ministry) on the altar, and it sustains only to the degree that God sovereignly chooses to keep it alive. When God is thus the source of our lives, we will no longer be looking to others to guarantee us a place within institutions of ministry. Herein we will find the true freedom of heart to be loyal to God's Davids without any strings attached.

### A Loyalty Story

A personal friend who is the Senior Pastor of a large church on the east coast told me a story that illustrated his understanding of what it means to be loyal to his leadership team. This story shows the personal nature of loyalty. I'm repeating it with his permission.

In the church where he is pastor, they encountered some significant financial challenges because of a certain outreach ministry in the church. It was estimated that the church would lose $500,000 over the course of the following year if the outreach was maintained. So the executive leadership team met to discuss what to do.

Everyone on the executive committee was saying they should shut down the outreach. My friend, the pastor, told them that in his opinion it was the worst thing to do. He reminded them of the assurances they had made to their congregation regarding that outreach, and that many of their members were with the church because of that ministry. He told them in the strongest terms possible that it would be a disastrous decision for the church if they shut down the outreach. He said they would be better off absorbing the $500,000 loss and staying in the good graces of their members. By folding the ministry outreach, my friend perceived that the backlash from the congregation would be much more devastating to the church over the long haul than if they just absorbed the $500,000 loss. He foresaw a potential $1 million loss to the church due to upset members leaving the church.

The other six members on the executive committee adamantly disagreed. They believed the only way to stop the hemorrhage was to terminate the outreach ministry. While my friend had the authority as pastor to make a unilateral decision, he would have had to do it in the face of direct resistance from his primary executive team, all of whom were his close friends. He protested their decision again and again, but since they were all unified so passionately in their determination to close down the ministry, my friend decided to defer to their judgment. He told them, "I assure you that this is going to be disastrous for our church, but I will go with you on this one because you are so strong in your unity."

But then he went on to say, "Now, here's how this works for me. Since I'm agreeing with you behind closed doors, from now on I lose my right to ever say, 'I told you so,' at any level, anywhere. Since I'm choosing to agree in private, I will always stand with you in this decision in public, even if there's a backlash from our congregation. That's what agreement means for me." For my friend, these were the implications of his loyalty to his friends on the leadership team. His loyalty to them meant he would stand with them, even if it was to his own hurt. He went on to say, "I'm going with it, but get ready, this is going to hurt."

So now to the rest of the story. When they announced the closing of the ministry outreach, the eruption of indignation from certain members in the congregation was astronomical. Some meetings were held with the church members to help them understand the decision, but due to schedule conflicts, the pastor was left to chair most of the meetings by himself. He ended up having to defend a decision he didn't even agree with.

The church members, however, turned it into a personal assault on the pastor. They spoke of promises he had personally made to them. They said, "How can you do this to us after we have been loyal to you over the years and have helped you get to where you are now?" It seemed to the people that the pastor had forsaken his loyalty to them for the sake of saving $500,000.

The pastor represented the decision in such a way that the congregation never got the slightest hint there was anything but full agreement at the executive committee level. He took the full heat from the church members for the decision, all the while agreeing inwardly with their complaint. To this day the members know no differently.

And as evidence of his loyalty to his friends on the executive committee, he has never once said to them, "I told you so." In my friend's opinion, being loyal to the executive committee meant standing in solidarity with their decision when the church members were attacking him, and then losing his right to throw it back in their faces. Incidentally, the church suffered a loss in excess of $1 million because of upset people who left the church.

### For Group Discussion

1. Review this chapter's story of the friend who was able to receive again from his pastor once he repented and returned to loyalty. Has anything similar ever happened to you?

2. What would you say is the stronger element for you: loyalty to your leader, or loyalty to your group (church, denomination, etc.)? Do you agree with the author's perspective that loyalty to an individual is the more desirable?

3. How do you feel about loyalty to a church or denomination? Is it desirable? To what measure?

4. Talk about the statement, "Loyalty means that we help each other obey God today." Is this kind of loyalty present in your group?

5. Talk about the closing story. Do you agree with how the Pastor chose to walk through the situation? Did he do right by honoring loyalty to his leaders even when the congregation felt he had been disloyal to them?

# CHAPTER 13

## A Loyal Spirit

*I*f loyalty is the fruit, a loyal spirit is the trunk and root. *A loyal spirit will always bear the fruit of loyalty.* Once a loyal spirit has been cultivated within, loyalty will manifest as an abundant harvest all one's days. The key, then, is to cultivate a loyal spirit within the heart.

A loyal spirit is a heart that is inclined to be loyal. All of us have seasons in our lives when we're not able to give our loyalty to the leader who is currently over us; however, a loyal spirit will mourn those seasons and yearn for things to change. And even when it cannot be loyal, a loyal spirit will never stoop to drink of the cup of disloyalty.

### God Is A Loyal Spirit

A loyal spirit is demonstrated for us first and foremost by God Himself. When we behold the loyalty within the Trinity for each other, we are empowered to pursue a loyal spirit. We pursue a loyal spirit because God is a loyal Spirit and we want to be just like Him.[1]

But God's loyalty isn't confined to the Trinity. When we believe in the Son of God for our salvation, God takes the fiery loyalty He has for His Son and transfers that same loyalty to us. When you love His Son, He loves you. His loyalty is so firm and His grip on our lives so steadfast that no one can snatch us out of our Father's hand.[2] And He Himself has said to us, "'Yes, I have loved you with an everlasting love'" (Jeremiah 31:3). His love for us is timeless, unchanging and eter-

[1] Matthew 5:48.
[2] John 10:29.

nal. Herein is loyalty at its highest and best!

### How Does God Measure A Loyal Spirit?

What criteria does God use to determine if someone has a loyal spirit? The answer may be surprising.

The evidence suggests that God evaluates the condition of our heart based upon our loyalty to one another. *God seems to view our loyalty to each other as the litmus test of whether we truly have a loyal spirit.*

How can one be loyal to God whom he has not seen, if he is not loyal to his brother whom he has seen?[3]

A loyal spirit desires to be loyal to both God and man. In fact, he who is loyal to God *will* be loyal to man.

There is one who says, "I am loyal to God alone; I will not give my loyalty to any man." On the surface that sounds noble because it appears to be free of the fear of man. But it's a cover for a disloyal spirit. Those who cannot give their heart in loyalty to man are deceived if they think they are altogether loyal to God.

Now, I recognize there are times when it becomes necessary to take a stand and distance ourselves from brethren in deception. But the heart of loyalty does so under extreme duress. A loyal spirit is grieved when loyalties must be severed and always prefers to find a way of reconciliation.

### A Loyal Spirit Is Consistently Loyal

I've noticed there are some people who just tend to be loyal, and others who find it difficult to be loyal. The difference is inside, and it has more to do with who they are internally than who others are who surround them externally.

*A loyal spirit tends to be loyal at multiple levels, with a variety of parties.* I've noticed that people with a loyal spirit will usually be loyal to their relationships at each phase of their journey. If they move to a new location, they quickly demonstrate the same loyalty to their new relationships that they evidenced in their previous locality. It hardly matters where you place them. Scatter them to the other side of the nation and then come back in a couple years—you will find them giv-

---

[3] "He who does not love his brother whom he has seen, how can he love God whom he has not seen?" (1 John 4:20).

ing loyal support to the work of God wherever they are. That's because those with a loyal spirit are readily loyal.

The opposite is also true. *A disloyal spirit seems incapable of finding a place where it can rest its loyalties.* Gene Edwards aptly wrote, "The Absaloms of this world can never see a David, they can see only Saul."[4] No church is ever right enough; no ministry is ever compelling enough; no leader is ever capable enough. They can be placed in the midst of thriving, healthy communities of believers but never find the inner capacity to give their hearts in true loyalty to those God has placed over them. An Absalom will always be disloyal, no matter which David you place him under.

Those who are loyal in one relationship will tend to be loyal in another. David seemed to really understand this, because he had the practice of honoring those who were loyal to his antagonists. When the men of Jabesh Gilead rescued Saul's body and buried him in loyalty, David sent them a note of commendation.[5] David was honoring of Abner, even though Abner's loyalties had been to Saul's house.[6] And then there's the real mysterious instance when David made Amasa the commander of his army after Amasa had been loyal to Absalom.[7] This pattern in David's behavior demonstrates that he valued a loyal spirit when he saw it, for he knew that a man who had been loyal once would be loyal again.

### How Does A Loyal Spirit Leave?

One of the most painful crossroads for the loyal spirit is when it must leave its leader for valid, understandable reasons. A loyal spirit will stay with David as long as possible. However, in some instances loyalty to God means that we must separate ourselves from the David of our local house because of improprieties or incompatibilities. To the loyal spirit, the paramount question is, "How do I separate myself properly in a way that pleases God?"

To answer that question, we must first understand an important distinction. There are not just two categories of people—the loyal and

[4] A Tale Of Three Kings, Gene Edwards, Auburn ME: Christian Books, 1980, p. 82.
[5] 2 Samuel 2:5-7.
[6] 2 Samuel 3.
[7] 2 Samuel 19:13.

the disloyal. *There is a third category: Those with an excellent spirit.* Many people fall into this category. I would define those with an excellent spirit as those who have not been given the gift of loyalty to their present leader, but who absolutely refuse to lower themselves to tramping the compromising marshland of disloyalty. They will never do anything to harm or undermine God's anointed.[8] Instead, they conduct themselves in uprightness and integrity in every way while under the leader's authority, and if they feel they must leave, they will do so graciously and with excellence.

Be sure you get this. *If you are not able to be loyal to a given leader, you need never drink of the cup of disloyalty.* You can—yes, you must—maintain an excellent spirit both while you stay and if you leave. Decide right now you will never stoop to disloyalty. Preserve your integrity.

If you leave a leader to whom you have been loyal, it does not automatically mean you are being disloyal. Leaving does not equal disloyalty. Sometimes we must leave. But it's essential *how* we leave. Even when a loyalty must be abandoned, a loyal spirit will conduct itself with integrity and nobility. An excellent spirit will do everything in its power to leave in a quiet, amicable manner. "If it is possible, as much as depends on you, live peaceably with all men" (Romans 12:18).

Disloyalty leaves a mess in its wake. Those who feel a mandate to warn others about the leader are rarely flowing in the Spirit of Christ. "They went out from us, but they were not of us; for if they had been of us, they would have continued with us; but they went out that they might be made manifest, that none of them were of us" (1 John 2:19).

It is possible, in a theoretical sense, to transfer your loyalties from one David to another David; however, if you do it with a loyal spirit, you will never be disloyal to the first David. You will simply separate yourself quietly without crossing over into disloyalty. *Disloyalty is not simply the discarding of a loyalty; it is the violating of a loyalty by undermining the credibility of the leader.*

Unfortunately, not all leaders understand the distinction between disloyalty and an excellent spirit, and in some systems it's almost impossible to leave without being dubbed a traitor. But a man with an excellent spirit will not slander upset leaders on his way out the door, even if he is being slandered himself.

---

[8] Psalm 105:15.

When is a true son justified in breaking off the affectionate allegiance he once gave to a spiritual father? Each situation is unique, so there are no clear rules. Generally, it may be necessary to sever loyalty when a leader takes a seriously wrong turn (doctrinally or ethically). Or, it may be necessary and prudent to leave a ministry if the favor of God has departed from that ministry. Sons or daughters who are grappling with these kinds of weighty decisions should not act in haste, but make their decisions in fasting and prayer and with sound counsel from an outside source. Find a seasoned leader who can give you wise counsel from the vantage of experience and impartiality.

What should we do if we feel the blessing of the Lord no longer rests on the leader or group to which we have been loyal for years? For starters, let's search our own hearts to be sure there isn't something amiss within us that keeps us from being rooted and fruitful. Let's not be "spiritual transients" in the body of Christ. Assuming that we've judged our own hearts adequately and still feel to leave, let me reiterate our earlier statement that loyalty is not unqualified allegiance. If God's blessing has been removed, and you have a release in your heart, it is not an act of disloyalty to leave. Leave with integrity and excellence. Having said that, I also recognize that God calls some to stay on a sinking ship. Many times we desperately need those who, through prayer, will be preserving elements in our historic churches. God can breathe life back into dead bones. Nothing shall be impossible with God!

### The Challenge of Leaving In A Right Way

My friends, the Rands,[9] found themselves facing the challenge of needing to leave their church but wanting to do it the right way. They were in their twenties, on staff at the church, and had come to the position bright-eyed and full of hope, expecting years of delightful ministry. But they were hardly three weeks in the new position before they knew it was not a good fit.

They simply did not connect with the pastor's leadership style. However, they had made a commitment to stay for at least a couple years and wanted to abide by that commitment. The longer they stayed, though, the more disturbed they became. They saw things in the way ministry was done that they felt were wrong, but knew it was

---

[9] Not their actual name.

not their place to attempt to address anything.

When they found themselves becoming cynical, they knew they had to get out for the sake of their spiritual health. They prayed fervently, and the Lord opened a door for them to move to another ministry opportunity several states away.

As they were leaving, my friends fought the temptation to express their concerns to some of the people in the church to whom they had gotten close and loved dearly. It was the proving of loyalty for them. Although they were never loyal in their hearts to the pastor (God had simply not given them that affectionate allegiance), they wanted to honor God by relating to the pastor with a loyal spirit. So they bit their tongues and left town without spreading anything that could have been considered slanderous or undermining.

When I consider where my friends were at that time in their lives, it's my conviction that they passed a certain test before God. They refused to drink the cup of disloyalty, even though they felt they had many valid concerns. I believe the Lord honored them for the way they maintained a loyal spirit, and He in turn made them leaders of their own team.

By the way, a year after the Rands left that church, it fragmented in many directions. There was no "split"; the people just scattered. They told me how grateful they were before the Lord that they personally had no hand in contributing to the collapse of that ministry. The Lord carried His people through it, and the vast majority of the believers were reconnected to other portions of the body of Christ. They told me, "The Lord taught us that we didn't have to campaign to protect God's people from controlling leadership styles; our duty before Him was to maintain a loyal spirit toward the pastor we were serving. God took care of His sheep."

### *For Group Discussion*

1.  What determines loyalty? Is it something that arises from within, or is it generated by external circumstances?
2.  Do you agree, that God measures our spirit, not by our loyalty to Him, but by our loyalty to each other?
3.  Have you known people who are loyal, no matter where they move, or where they go? Tell the group about them.
4.  Talk about the right way and the wrong way to leave a team. How would you handle it if someone on your team decided to leave?

# CHAPTER 14

## *Loyalty To Authority*

*T*he challenge of loyalty is "upward." By that I mean, loyalty is the most difficult—and the most dazzling—when it's directed to those who have authority over us. Perhaps it's someone who holds a position over us organizationally, such as a boss; or someone who is relationally over us, such as a parent; or someone who is over us in terms of spiritual authority, such as a pastor. *When someone has authority over your life, that's when you find out whether you have a loyal spirit.*

Absalom felt loyal in his heart to the men of Israel, demonstrated very graphically by the way he gave them personal affection and attention. He was even loyal to his siblings. But his loyalty was not going to be measured by his relationship with his peers (siblings) or those under him (the men of Israel); his loyalty was going to be defined by his heart attitudes toward the one man who was *over* him—his father David. Even though Absalom showed loyalty to many, he has gone down in the annals of history as the quintessential example of disloyalty because he was disloyal to the one man who was *over* him (David).

There is a peer-level loyalty that is wonderful and commendable, such as the loyalty between siblings, or between friends (an example being David and Jonathan's relationship). Peer-level loyalty also exists between members of a team. Team loyalty is necessary for healthy ministry, since ministry is essentially collegial rather than individual. Loyalty at the peer level is easy to embrace, however, because the peer has no authority over us. For example, Apollos was Paul's peer, so when Paul urged him to go to a certain place at a certain time, Apollos was able to gracefully refuse without his loyalty coming into question. Timothy, in contrast, was not Paul's peer, but was "under" Paul as his spiritual son. So for Timothy to refuse Paul would have constituted a breach of loyalty.

We may claim to be loyal to someone who is under us, such as an employee, but it's easy to feel loyal to someone who has absolutely no power or right to call us to account. For example, Paul might say that he was loyal to Timothy, but in reality that loyalty would have a low price tag because Timothy would never presume to tell Paul what to do.

*All the rules of loyalty change when it involves relating to someone who has authority over our lives.* It's here that loyalty is truly tested, and it's here alone that loyalty is seen in its pristine beauty and magnificence. This is why Timothy was commended as a "true son" by Paul, for he had proven his loyalty to Paul by being obedient to Paul's oversight. The rub in loyalty is not for the father in relating to the son, but for the son in relating to the father. It is the rub of coming under the egis[1] of the one whose sphere includes you.

Thus, bosses don't struggle with being loyal to their employees; their challenge is with their own boss. Similarly, home group leaders don't struggle with being loyal to their group attendees; their challenge is to be loyal to their pastor. Likewise, pastors don't struggle with being loyal to their flock, or even to pastors of other churches; their struggle has more to do with relating to their apostolic covering or denominational overseers.

### Loyalty To Those Over Us

The Bible calls us to be loyal to those who are over us in the Lord. For example, when David was king over the people of Israel, Scripture commended those who were loyal to him:

> All these men of war, who could keep ranks, came to Hebron with a loyal heart, to make David king over all Israel (1 Chronicles 12:38).

> But the men of Judah, from the Jordan as far as Jerusalem, remained loyal to their king (2 Samuel 20:2).

---

[1] Egis (or aegis) refers to the orb over which one has a protecting influence. We are using the word, in this book, to speak of the sphere within which one has spiritual authority.

The men of war were loyal to God's man. Their example compels us. So when God places you under a David, be loyal to him or her!

These same principles apply in the business community. If you're an employee and you have a compassionate boss, it is commendable to be a loyal employee. Similarly, wise employers will be on the lookout for those employees who evidence a loyal spirit. You can't buy a loyal spirit by paying an employee more. But surely it would be appropriate to reward a loyal spirit with promotions and pay increases, because those with a loyal spirit are those with whom you can build a long-term team network.

### David Was Loyal To His Father

There's a reason why the Spirit of God gave David's followers a heart of loyalty for their leader. It was because David had first of all proved that he himself had a loyal spirit. This was proven at a time in his life when he didn't even realize he was undergoing a test.

The test came in his teen years, while he was tending his father's sheep. They weren't his sheep; they were his father's. As such, it could have been tempting for David to adopt a little bit of a hireling spirit. He could have thought to himself, "I'm going to watch over these sheep because it's my job, but I'm certainly not going to kill myself to take care of them. After all, bottom line they're not my ultimate responsibility, they're my father's. So I'll do what's expected of me, but I'm not going to get myself killed for a bunch of sheep that aren't even mine."

But David didn't think like that. He was a true shepherd to the sheep because he was loyal to his father. *Loyalty is not loyalty, however, until it is proven in the crucible of crisis.* And David's loyalty to his father was about to be tested. The test came in the form of a lion and a bear. On two separate occasions, a lion and a bear came and grabbed a lamb from the flock and headed for cover. It would have been humanly understandable for a young shepherd-son to report to his father, "Dad, a lion came and grabbed one of the lambs, and there was nothing I could do. I shouted; I threw some rocks at it with my sling; but I couldn't stop the lion from running off with the lamb. Sorry, Dad, but the lamb is gone."

David brought no such report to his father, however, for he was no hireling. Instead, he put his life on the line. He basically said to the lion and the bear, "Over my dead body!" He risked his neck to save a lamb. The Bible says that David rose and ran after the beast and struck

93

it until it let go of the lamb. Then, when the beast turned on him, he grabbed it by its beard and struck and killed it.[2] In this manner, he killed both a lion and a bear.

There's no way to prepare yourself to fend off a lion or to kill a bear. It's not as though you can rent a lion for a day and practice killing it. In killing the lion and the bear, David was stepping onto a totally untested battlefield (a move that would serve him well in his upcoming fight with Goliath). The risk of running to the rescue of the lamb was extremely high. Out of loyalty to his father, David took his very life into his own hands.

When God saw this kind of loyalty in David, God realized that he had a loyal spirit. Thus, He chose David to come into a place of unique intimacy with Him. God saw in David a man who would remain loyal to Him, even in the face of accusation. Furthermore, God established him as the man who would embody the scriptural principles of loyalty. David's life story is a gripping tale that illustrates the power of loyalty. Those who were loyal to David came into God's favor and blessing; those who were disloyal to David suffered the consequences of God's displeasure. Since David was loyal to his natural father and also to his God, God required others to be loyal to him.

This makes me take inventory: Do I have the heart of David? Have I proven my loyalty to my father and/or mother?

### Why David Is A Safe Leader

Loyalty is *always* risky. However, some leaders are safer than others. Being under David is risky, but not as much as being under Saul. David represents the leader who is safest to follow because he is first and foremost a lover of God, and secondarily a lover of men. David has the first commandment in first place, so he serves before God with a happy heart. His mood is dictated by his vertical relationship, not his horizontal relationships. Because he is a lover of God, he will lay his life down for the sheep. This makes him safe to follow.

David is safe because he's learned how to walk gracefully in seasons of loss or diminishment. The same heart was in John the Baptist. When Jesus showed up and drew all the crowds away from John's meetings, John's response was, "'Therefore this joy of mine is ful-

---

[2] See 1 Samuel 17:34-35.

filled'" (John 3:29). All John wanted to do was direct the hearts of men away from himself and onto the beloved Bridegroom. *When a leader remains lovesick for Christ in the midst of personal diminishment, you know he or she is safe to follow in loyalty because he or she is not motivated by personal ambitions but by intimacy.*

David may have many Kingdom mandates, but he has only one agenda. His only agenda is to gain Christ—and since you can't help or hinder his agenda, you are safest under his leadership. Whatever building David does (such as the building of a ministry, or of temporal structures) is not a reflection of his *agenda* but his *mandates.* David does a *lot* of building because of his calling, but he doesn't gain his personal identity from what he builds, so he doesn't usurp the needy in the process. He satisfies his need for personal identity through his *pursuit* of Christ, not through his *projects.* David has a cry that is clearly beheld by his observers, "I have got to get Him. I have got to behold Him. I have got to apprehend Him. I have got to know Him!" *It's this pursuit of the excellence of the knowledge of Christ that makes David safe to follow.* Why? Because people are not a means to his end. What he's after cannot be enhanced by gathering more people around him. *A leader is safest to follow when no follower can help or hinder his inner heart agenda, because his inner agenda is to seek and gain Christ.*

It wasn't David's superior people skills that made him safe, because his history proved he lacked people skills. It was his heart after God that made him safe. Absalom didn't think, however, that David was safe at all. He felt violated and ignored by David. But in the final analysis, the problem was not David's poor people skills but Absalom's bitter spirit. *David handled Absalom imperfectly but kept chasing God; Absalom responded imperfectly but grew bitter because of his self-seeking motives that weren't brought to the cross.*

One of the primary elements that determines how safe a leader is to follow is how that leader handles his or her insecurities. Generally, insecurities are inner self-protecting mechanisms that usually remain hidden until times of crisis, confrontation, stress, or diminishment. Like every leader, David had his insecurities; but he learned to present them to his God and allow God to fight for him.[3] David refused to fight for himself. Saul, on the other hand, could never face his insecurities,

---

[3] For example, see 1 Samuel 30:6.

so he became a self-preserving leader. *The fruit of self-loyalty is self-preservation. Self-preservation ultimately ends in the quest to eliminate someone else.* The instinct for self-preservation is within all of us. All of us have the potential to be a Saul or a David. Sometimes we move back and forth between them—we get in a servant mode, and then fall back into self-preservation. *The mark of loyalty to God is that we relinquish our grip on self-preservation.* David found a way to bring his insecurities before God and lay them to rest in the magnificence of beholding the excellent Majesty. You're safest in submitting to leaders who have found a way to get their insecurities settled in the love of God. Leaders who are confident in love know that God will grant them their destined status among men; they don't have to elbow their way into their placement.

One of the great crises in the church today is leaders who have not had their insecurities settled in the place of intimacy with Jesus—hearing the Bridegroom's voice—and finding all their longings and desires fulfilled in His presence. Rather than having their identity established in Christ, such leaders often find their identity in their relationship with the Lamb's Wife, the Bride, and view believers as a resource base to fulfill their vision. Those who give their loyalties to such leaders run the risk of eventually feeling manipulated or usurped.

Most saints in the body of Christ are longing to give their heart in loyalty to one of God's Davids, but the sad truth is that not every gifted, anointed leader in the body of Christ has the heart of David. Some leaders are motivated, often subconsciously, by desires for personal significance and visible accomplishments. People become a means to help them fulfill their goals. Anointed leaders with ministry-building goals are not as safe to follow for two reasons: *Firstly, they are needing people to gather around them in order to fulfill their goals.* When they don't meet their goals or expectations, their tendency is to place the fault with their followers. In frustration, they sometimes handle the people in a way that produces disillusionment and hurt. *Secondly, when they look to ministry accomplishments for their sense of identity and fulfillment, God Himself resists them because their self-identity is built on a faulty foundation.*

As a word of balance, beware of adopting a policeman attitude in the body of Christ that goes around trying to figure out who is David and who is not. This was Gene Edwards' warning when he wrote, "Men who go after the Sauls among us often crucify the Davids among us."[4]

"It seems to me that's a kingdom-builder over there." "That's a man with an agenda." "Oh-oh, watch out for that sister, she's trying to build something." Start to meddle like that in the body of Christ and God will resist *you*. Instead, let your prayer be, "God, make *me* a David! Give *me* an undivided heart to fear Your name!"

### *"But My Leader Isn't As Wonderful As David Was"*

It's easy to think, "I would have been loyal had I been under King David. But the fact is, the one I'm under is no David." We assume that David was such a wonderful leader that it was *easy* to be loyal to him. Truth be known, David had more uprisings against his leadership than most of the other kings in the Bible. Not everybody had it in their hearts to be loyal to David. Those on a search for David's flaws didn't have far to look.

*In all honesty, all human leaders have areas of brokenness and weakness and dysfunction in their leadership styles and abilities.* Although they do their best, they still disappoint. Many people become disloyal to their leader because they discern his or her weaknesses. If you wait for a leader to be deserving of your loyalty, however—that is, if you wait for a leader who will treat you the way you like to be treated—you run the risk of never being loyal to anyone.

A loyal spirit is loyal to its leader, not because it has been handled perfectly, but because God has joined its heart to the leader in the Spirit. *A loyal spirit recognizes that, even though a certain leader has weaknesses, the hand of God is still upon him or her for good.* So the loyal spirit will benefit from partnering with the leader and will share in a dimension of fruitfulness that will be lacking in the life of the one who couldn't walk with that leader anymore. The disloyal person feels justified in parting company, but at the end of the day it's the measure of fruitfulness in our lives that determines the wisdom of our choices. *Loyalty consistently bears more fruit.*

We typically think that the presence of loyalty is determined by the leader. That is, if the leader is deserving, he or she will earn the

[4] A Tale Of Three Kings, Gene Edwards, Auburn ME: Christian Books, 1980, p. 44.

loyalty of others. But I'm suggesting that the presence of loyalty is more a function of the *follower* than the *leader*. Loyalty is based not so much upon the leader's prowess as it is based upon whether the follower has a loyal spirit.

The same principle holds true in marriage: The power of loyalty derives from within. Those who are true to their marital vows are not loyal because they married the perfect spouse, but because they have a true, noble heart. A loyal man is true to his wife, not because of who *she* is, but because of who *he* is. A man might argue, "I was not faithful to my wife because she was a pain to live with." To which I would respond, don't make your disloyalty the other person's problem. Your disloyalty is not because of something in her, but because of something in you. A loyal spirit finds its impetus from within.

The great question is, "Do I have a loyal spirit? First to God, and then to David?" A loyal spirit will weather the turbulence of David's foibles and persevere to the end, ultimately sharing in the glory of David's conquests.

### *For Group Discussion*

1. Discuss this statement, "We haven't truly determined whether we have a loyal spirit until we examine the way we relate to those who are over us." When you examine yourself, what are your conclusions?

2. Have there been times when your loyalty was being tested, and you didn't even realize it until later? Share an experience.

3. Our chapter says, "If you wait for a leader to be deserving of your loyalty—that is, if you wait for a leader who will treat you the way you like to be treated—you run the risk of never being loyal to anyone." Would you agree? Do you have a situation in mind to support your opinion?

4. Do you agree with the author's distinction between *agenda* and *mandate*? How would you describe your personal agenda and mandates?

5. Let's talk about our insecurities. What are our self-preserving instincts that keep us from being Davidic leaders?

6. We said it was David's heart after God that made him a safe leader to follow. How has this statement challenged your priorities as a leader? Talk about your desire to be a David.

# CHAPTER 15

# *The Basis Of Loyalty*

S o the question is of paramount importance: How do we
determine to whom we'll give our loyalties? All of us want
to be loyal, but what criteria should we use in deciding to
whom to be loyal?

I see six general reasons why we might be loyal to someone.

- Loyalty is based upon a history of proven relationship.
- Loyalty is based upon covenant.
- Loyalty is based on the conviction that God is loyal to that David.
- Loyalty to David is rooted in a desire to share in the promises made to David.
- Loyalty is based upon a true father/son connection.
- God expects a loyal spirit when he places someone over your life.

### *Loyalty Is Based Upon A History Of Proven Relationship*

When people have proven themselves to you over the years as
being dependable, selfless, nurturing, giving, and serving, then it's
understandable that you would give your loyalty to them. Take your
parents, for example. If they were tender and upright with you during
your upbringing, you probably became loyal to them. You'll stand with
them now through virtually any challenge because they stood with you
all those years. The Lord delights in this kind of loyalty to parents,
conferring upon it the blessing of a long life.[1]

[1] Ephesians 6:3.

*Loyalty is a family thing.* It's something that flows between sons and fathers, between daughters and mothers. It's in the genes; it's a DNA connection.

There is loyalty between brothers and sisters, but it's different than that between sons and fathers. Siblings will stand at your side in loyalty, but they will not come under your authority. It's your sons and daughters that will come under your authority and covering of blessing. The loyalty of peer friendship is sweet, but a peer relationship keeps friends plowing in separate fields. The thing that builds the Kingdom is the loyalty of sons walking in submission to the fathers, because the sons will come and plow together with the fathers.

The only time brothers will plow together is if it is under the egis of their common father. If there is no father present to galvanize the sons, the sons will separate. More can be accomplished, however, when brothers join together toward a common vision. This is why fathers are so important; they become the glue that keeps the sons building together, growing together, and working together. *When fathers are in place, with their sons gathered about them, the Kingdom of God enjoys its greatest expansion. Where fathers are lacking the sons tend to disperse, causing the total impact of their efforts to be diffused and diminished.*

Often our loyalty to spiritual parents is based upon their faithfulness in nurturing us. You may consider someone your spiritual father or mother because that person led you to the Lord, or has fed you in your Christian walk, or has served to establish your heart in faith and love. He or she has proved to be a true shepherd, not a hireling. When someone has made a profound spiritual impact in your life, it's quite natural to find yourself being loyal to that person. His or her impartation into your life was a watershed experience. Loyalty will never deny that kind of powerful history with a father or mother in the faith.

Paul appealed to the Corinthians to give their hearts in loyalty to his oversight, an appeal that was expressed repeatedly in his second letter to that church. He cited his history of ministry in their midst as a fitting basis for their loyalty. "You are our epistle written in our hearts, known and read by all men; clearly you are an epistle of Christ, ministered by us, written not with ink but by the Spirit of the living God, not on tablets of stone but on tablets of flesh, that is, of the heart" (2 Corinthians 3:2-3). Paul had proven his care for them, and now he considered their loyalty to be a fitting response.

*Loyalty usually exists where followers have an appreciation for the leadership style of the leader.* It has judged the leader to be sincere, trustworthy, safe, holding favor with God, pursuing goals and values we also want to pursue, and doing it in a way that wins our approval. Loyalty says, "I like where you're headed, and I appreciate the way you're going about it; I want to go with you."

Loyalty has joined its heart to David because it has come to trust the heart motives of David. Even though David is not perfect, loyalty has determined that David's motives are noble. Although David may hurt you, David will never *intend* to hurt you. So when David's motives appear questionable, loyalty can say, "I know he would never mean to do what you think he's done. I've been with him long enough to know he never meant to hurt you."

David has proven over time that he is a good shepherd. "'The good shepherd gives his life for the sheep'" (John 10:11). His care for the flock comes before personal agendas. David does not trust his own heart, but lives in the realization that he himself is a broken leader. One thing that makes him safe is that he is more concerned about pleasing God than pleasing people. Time has proven the authenticity of David's heart and motives, and now your heart has formed an affectionate allegiance.

My friend, Paul Johansson, tells a great story about loyalty that goes back to his years serving as a missionary in Nairobi, Kenya, where he launched a Bible School in 1967. As President, it was his responsibility to find a cook for the school. He asked around, and finally someone told him they knew of a good cook who had served in the local hospital. There was only one problem—he was in jail. So Paul went down to the local jail and said to the officer at the front desk, "I want to see Elias Irungu." He heard the cell doors clang open, and a tall, balding man appeared at the counter. Paul asked, "What was your crime?" Elias said that while working in the hospital, there were two occasions when he had to rebuke the senior cook because he saw "the devil in his eyes." The second time he did it, Elias had a knife in his hand, which almost gave the senior cook a heart attack on the spot. So Elias was immediately locked up. Paul said to the officer, "This is my friend. I will take him with me." Paul signed the register and took him out (obviously this didn't happen in America!). Paul took him from the jail, set him up with lodging at the Bible School, and installed him as the school cook. Paul told me, "He was the most trusted and loyal worker I had." Occasionally, Elias would rebuke the students, and the other missionaries would want Paul to fire him. But Paul said, "No, as long as I am here, he is with me." After Paul returned to America, he would occasionally visit the work in Africa, and of course see how Elias was doing. And there he was, still cooking faithfully, and still thankful that Paul had gotten him out of jail. Paul proved his goodwill toward Elias, and now he had a lifelong friend. Elias recently retired after 31 years of cooking. Paul summarized their relationship this way: "Loyal to the end, and still my friend." Elias's loyalty was based on a proven history together.

### Loyalty Is Based Upon Covenant

Not all forms of loyalty are based upon covenant, but some forms are. Take, for example, that which exists in marriage. There's a loyalty in marriage based upon the fact that two people have made an altar before God and come into covenant relationship. There's a line in the traditional wedding vows that says, "And thereto I pledge thee my troth." That's actually a vow of loyalty to each other. "For better, for worse" means that couples commit to being loyal to each other amidst the vicissitudes of life.

The loyalty that exists in marriage is truly remarkable. It causes people to cast aside any competing affections and devote their hearts in fidelity to just one person.

I have known people who have remained loyal to their spouse even after that spouse has been unfaithful to the marriage vows. They have been violated and spurned, and yet their loyalty oftentimes remains. It's an incredible thing to behold!

There's also a loyalty that believers hold toward one another that is rooted in covenant—in the New Covenant. The Lord's Supper is a covenant meal that confirms this loyalty. We celebrate the fact that we have come into covenant with God and with our fellow believers. We remember that we are all joined to one another—"For we, though many, are one bread and one body; for we all partake of that one bread" (1 Corinthians 10:17). As such, it's a loyalty meal, celebrating our loyalty to the catholic[2] body of Christ and to our Lord Himself. Paul pointed to this when he reminded them of the context of the first Supper: "The Lord Jesus on the same night in which He was betrayed took bread" (1 Corinthians 11:23). Jesus served the meal in the context of betrayal. Every time we eat the Lord's Supper, we honor our union with our brothers and sisters, and declare that betrayal has no place around this meal. The one who eats with betrayal and disloyalty in his heart "eats and drinks judgment to himself, not discerning the Lord's body" (1 Corinthians 11:29).

But now I want to make a distinction. There is a difference between being loyal to the universal body of Christ, and expressing loyalty to a specific church. *It's right for us to express a covenant of loyalty to the body of Jesus Christ through the Lord's Supper; but it's dangerous to invoke a covenant when expressing loyalty to a specific congregation or leader.* It's good to express *commitment* to your local church; but a *covenant* of loyalty can be a set-up for unnecessary wounding.

Within the church of Jesus Christ, I am persuaded it is dangerous to invoke a marriage-like covenant in order to elicit loyalty from believers to a local church. I was in a church once that had a covenant statement for its church members to sign, which was viewed as an expression of loyalty to each other. Evaluating that approach years later, the fruit from that brand of covenantal loyalty was not positive. It set people up for wounding and failure. In instances where the covenant collapsed, saints were riven with condemnation and accusation.

So covenant as a basis for loyalty is best kept within marriage. But there may be one exception in the church. When a pastor or ministry leader is hiring others to assist him or her in the work of the ministry, it's understandable for that leader to desire loyalty from those on his or her paid staff. It would be fitting for a staff member to say to the leader, "I covenant to be loyal to you as long as I am on your ministry staff. If my loyalty should ever depart, then I will resign my position." The last thing a loyal spirit wants to do is remain on staff in a ministry where loyalties have dissipated. And during the transition period, the last thing a loyal spirit will do is be disloyal to the leader while on the way out the door.

---

[2] "Catholic" means "universal."

### Loyalty Is Based On The Conviction That God Is Loyal To That David

While I am loyal to Jesus for what He has done for me in purchasing my redemption, I am also loyal to Him for this simple reason: God the Father is loyal to Him. *I want to be loyal to whomever the Father is loyal to.* I know that the Father is so loyal to Jesus that He is going to make Jesus' enemies a footstool for His feet. Nothing can stop that divine determination. So my loyalty is with Jesus because I know that those who are loyal to Him will share in His triumph.

In a similar way, I want to be loyal to those leaders to whom I believe God is loyal. If God is their friend, I want to be their friend. If God fights their battles, I'm going to be on their side. If God likes them, then I want to like them too.

David remained loyal to his God[3]—even through the wilderness of shattered dreams. So God was loyal to David. I believe we can invoke the principle of Psalm 18:25 and say, to the loyal He shows Himself loyal. God shows Himself loyal to those who have demonstrated their loyalty to Him.

When you find a David, be loyal to him or her. When you find a David whose heart is resolute in seeking God, you're safest in giving your loyalty to that David because God Himself is loyal to His Davids. If you're hesitant because your loyalty was violated in the past, then cry out to God for grace because it's time to love again.

A primary reason God was loyal to David was because David's foundational priority was intimacy with God. In the good times he wasn't distracted from keeping the face of God his primary pursuit. And when times got tough, David always reclused to the secret place of the Most High. He allowed neither bane nor blessing to derail his loyalty to God. In response, God stood by David in a most uncommon way.

When you know God is loyal to your David, your heart will be able to rest through those seasons when David makes dumb decisions. Even though David made some wrong choices, God was determined to bring him through to the other side of the mess. You're not loyal to David because you think he's perfect, but because you know God is com-

[3] 1 Kings 11:4.

mitted to leading him through the process of repentance, discipline, and restoration. Even if he falls seven times, David will certainly rise to his destiny.[4] So loyalty decides, "I think God likes this man. God is with him. God fights for him. I want to be on his side." When we see God's loyalty to David, it empowers our loyalty to David.

Some people become loyal to a leader because they are impressed with his or her giftings, or anointing, or winsome personality, or ability to build. But this is a faulty basis for loyalty. Just because a leader has strong giftings does not necessarily mean he has developed the kind of inner character that gains God's smile. Instead of asking, "Is this a capable leader?" we should be asking, "Is God loyal to this leader?"

Once again let me quote Amasai's utterance of loyalty: "'We are yours, O David; we are on your side, O son of Jesse! Peace, peace to you, and peace to your helpers! For your God helps you'" (1 Chronicles 12:18). The reason for Amasai's loyalty is given in these simple words, "'For your God helps you.'" These words were not a statement of personal opinion, they were a prophetic declaration of divine truth. God was on David's side, working with him and for him in all things. Amasai and his followers recognized this and so they joined their hearts to David because they wanted to be where God was working.

*Smart warriors recognize that you don't necessarily want to be in the army that has the most warriors; you want to be in the army that is helped by God!* So even if David is holed up in a cave and living in reproach, loyalty is convinced God will bring him through. When you find a David who is helped by God, wisdom would suggest that you join your heart to his.

### Loyalty To David Is Rooted In A Desire To Share In The Promises Made To David

*One mark of those to whom God is loyal is that He tends to make great promises—even seemingly unconditional promises—to them.* That's both glorious and terrifying. Terrifying—because we serve a God who is radically resolute to fulfill His purpose and bring us to His determined end; and glorious—because "all the promises of God in Him are Yes, and in Him Amen, to the glory of God through us" (2 Corinthians 1:20). *Loyalty is wise enough to see the glorious promises of God given to one*

---

[4] Proverbs 24:16.

*of His Davids and say, "I want in."*

When Abner was attempting to rally the loyalties of the people of Israel back to David, he did so by reiterating God's promises to David.[5] The people gathered to David because they believed the promises.

God has given uncommon promises of Kingdom conquest to David, and loyalty aligns itself with David because it recognizes that God is in covenant with him. When you find yourself under the leadership of one of God's Davids, believe in the promises of God, and you will enjoy their fulfillment along with David.

Promises are rarely given to groups or institutions; they are usually given to a man or woman. *Loyalty believes in God's promise; therefore, loyalty is an expression of faith.* When the leader gets the promise, all those who have stood with that leader will also share in the promise. If you lose faith and transfer your loyalties to another leader, you will then become an heir to the promises given to that other leader; and you will forego the blessings promised to the former leader. So one of the issues of loyalty is, in whose promises do you want to share?

Twice in David's reign, people had to choose between David and one of his sons. Would they choose David or Absalom? David or Adonijah? Those who made the wrong choice often found it deadly. When we are forced to choose loyalties, we are probably at a very important crossroads of our life. Our choice may affect the rest of our destiny in God. When loyalties are chosen, it can be years before the fruit of one's decision is fully manifest. The wisdom of going with David, however, will eventually surface. *My advice: Go with the man who has the promise. Absalom had charisma, but David had promise.*

Lot is an example of a man who lightly esteemed the promises God gave to His servant Abraham. As Abraham's nephew, Lot was loyal to Abraham for many years. As long as he remained under the orb of Abraham's covering, Lot enjoyed great blessings. But it appeared that as Lot prospered, he began to develop negative attitudes toward Abraham. He was blessed because of his affiliation with Abraham, but it was those very blessings that turned his heart away from Abraham. Strife entered their relationship. As a reminder, here's the account of it.

[5] 2 Samuel 3:17-18.

Now the land was not able to support them, that they might dwell together, for their possessions were so great that they could not dwell together. And there was strife between the herdsmen of Abram's livestock and the herdsmen of Lot's livestock. The Canaanites and the Perizzites then dwelt in the land. So Abram said to Lot, "Please let there be no strife between you and me, and between my herdsmen and your herdsmen; for we are brethren. Is not the whole land before you? Please separate from me. If you take the left, then I will go to the right; or, if you go to the right, then I will go to the left" (Genesis 13:6-9).

Scripture is very discreet on the nature of this confrontation, so we don't know what all the issues were, nor who was right or wrong. If we knew the whole story, we would possibly learn that Abraham had disappointed Lot in some way. But whether Lot's grievance was valid or not, Abraham was a man with promises from God, and Lot didn't honor that fact sufficiently.

In order to resolve the growing strife with Lot and his herdsmen, Abraham suggested Lot move away in the direction of his choice, while Abraham would move in the opposite direction. Lot took the more pleasant plain, while Abraham went off to the rugged mountains. Lot had the better living situation but Abraham had the promises. By the time the story was finished, Lot was holed up in a cave with his two daughters, destitute of his wife and all his possessions, while Abraham was sitting in abundance with a miracle boy (Isaac) in his arms.

The Bible doesn't tell us Lot was disloyal to Abraham, so why would I suggest something like that? Because when everything went sour for Lot, and he ended up destitute and in a mountain cave, if he had remained loyal in his heart he could have returned to Abraham. But because of his bitterness, he was never able to return to his spiritual father. Disloyalty had wedged its diabolical work in Lot's soul, and in his hour of need he was unable to return to what could have been a homecoming of blessing and restoration. Disloyalty would not allow him to return to the man with the promises.

Lot's example demonstrates that once violated, loyalty is very difficult to recover. Disloyalty rarely returns to loyalty. Even though Abraham had saved Lot and his household in battle,[6] and even though

---

[6] Genesis 14.

Abraham had interceded for him when God was about to destroy So-dom,[7] Lot could not return to Abraham in his heart. Abraham continued to love, but Lot had lost his love. Once it was gone, loyalty was lost forever. And Lot paid dearly for it.

Peter calls Lot a righteous man,[8] so the issue with Lot was not whether he was righteous before God, nor was it whether he would share an eternal inheritance in the Kingdom of God. Disloyalty did not cause him to lose his salvation; but it did cause him to forfeit Kingdom blessings. The gravest consequences of his disloyalty were not reaped in his own life but in his offspring. As a result of the path that Lot took of separating himself from God's friend, his offspring became those who rallied other nations to persecute the people of God. Jesus said, "'But wisdom is justified by all her children'" (Luke 7:35). In other words, the wisdom of one's choices is not always manifest until the fruit is beheld in the lives of one's children. The wisdom of Lot's turning away from Abraham is seen in the path of his two sons. The nations that were birthed out of his two sons, Ammon and Moab, organized a confederacy to oppose Israel[9] and became historic persecutors of the people of God. The problem, it seems, is that Lot lost faith in the promises given to Abraham.

When there is strife between leaders on the same leadership team, they will sometimes seek help by calling in denominational leaders or neutral leaders who are esteemed by both parties. There are two primary questions adjudicating mediators seek to discern: To what degree is each party operating in the spirit of truth? And to what degree is each party operating in a spirit of love? The first question seeks to discern who is right and who is wrong; the second looks at the spirit in which the parties are operating. It's possible for Abraham to make some mistakes but yet be blessed of God because he is operating in love. It's important to God who is right and who is wrong, but it's even more important that we love one another. Abraham deferred to and preferred Lot, demonstrating the kind of character that delighted God's heart. That's one reason God was so pleased to extend such fantastic promises to Abraham. Unfortunately, Lot did not share in those promises.

[7] Genesis 18.
[8] 2 Peter 2:8.
[9] Psalm 83:5,8.

### Loyalty Is Based Upon A True Father/Son Connection

Happy is the son to whom God gives a genuine spiritual father—a father with an enlarged heart to help his sons into their fullest destiny. Happier still is that son when God empowers him to be a true son to that father.

Not all sons are true sons. Absalom was a natural son to David, but he was not a true son. A true son is a loyal son. Even though he was David's flesh and blood, Absalom was not a true, loyal son.

The expression "true son" was coined by Paul as he spoke regarding two of his sons in the faith.

> To Timothy, *a true son* in the faith (1 Timothy 1:2).
> To Titus, *a true son* in our common faith (Titus 1:4).

Timothy and Titus were both true sons to Paul—i.e., they had proven their loyalty to him over time. Paul didn't call Timothy a true son because he had led Timothy to Christ; in actuality, Timothy was a believer before he met Paul. So Paul wasn't saying, "You're my true son because I led you in the sinner's prayer." Rather, he was saying, "You're my true son because, when circumstances arose that challenged your fidelity, you proved your allegiance by remaining true to me. You've passed the test. Now I know that you will always be faithful and loving to me."

One of the marks of greatness is when a leader has the ability to gather others around him who are loyal to him. I've known some fathers in the faith who have an unusual magnetism and who draw sons to themselves—sons who are anxious to be fathered and who long to be true sons. No one can make this kind of a father. You can "make disciples" (Matthew 28:19), but you can't make spiritual fathers. Only God can make a father, forming and fashioning him in the crucible of His refining fires.

Absalom, Adonijah, and Solomon were all congenital sons of David, but of the three only Solomon was loyal. Some of the most godly kings among David's descendants (most notably Jehoshaphat and Hezekiah) made their greatest mistake in automatically installing their firstborn as king, using no other discernment in the selection process than the fact that he was the eldest. This produced great chaos in the land. David, in contrast, installed Solomon because of his loyalty.

Before his crowning, Solomon showed his loyalty by patiently waiting for David to initiate the coronation.

A true father or mother uses his or her personal resources to help the sons or daughters find their own destiny and purpose. They are even willing to suffer loss for the sake of the sons and daughters. This selflessness will cause the sons and daughters to give their hearts in loyalty. On the other hand, if a father is using his sons as a means to further his own agenda, the sons will pick up on that rather quickly and withdraw.

To be an effective father, it is essential that a father have his years of self-enrichment. Why? He must have something to give, something to pass along to the next generation. Some fathers never enter into true spiritual fatherhood because they were never successful at self-enrichment.

A common scenario in the church is to see those who wanted to be spiritual fathers and mothers, but they got so focused on the pursuit of self-enrichment that they lost perspective on why they were getting enriched. They became self-absorbed and failed to use their resources to empower the sons and daughters. There must come the time of transition when they get off the treadmill of self-enrichment and turn their hearts toward the children.

David was committed to using his own resources to enrich his men's lives. He committed the vastness of his resources to their stewardship, making them captains of fifties, hundreds, and thousands. They in turn gave themselves to protecting David, knowing that in David's blessing they would be blessed—because David shares everything.

God, give us such Davids today—fathers who enrich their sons through joint exploits! Better yet, Lord, make *me* into this kind of a David.

It's not that the father impoverishes himself for the sake of his sons. If the father is impoverished, he loses the very resource base that empowers him to give something to the next generation. Sons don't want an impoverished father, but they do want a father who is willing to divest himself in order to enrich the sons.

When a father is enriched and enthroned as a David in his own kingdom, his sons glory in his accomplishments.[10] Sons love to boast in the good name of their father.[11] The fathers, in turn, delight to boast in their children.[12]

When a son with a loyal spirit finds a father who will divest himself in order to endow the son, the son will be true for the rest of their years together. Investing in the son actually diminishes the father's resources, but he has the joy of watching the son begin to enter into his own. And the son is grateful in loyalty because he knows he would not be this far along in his journey without the father's endowment. A bond of love has formed between them, producing an affectionate allegiance. *Ultimately, the father's example in endowing his true son will empower the son to rise in his own right as an endowing father to the subsequent generation.*

### God Expects A Loyal Spirit When He Places Someone Over Your Life

*If God places you in a certain job, He expects you to show a loyal spirit toward your boss.* Even if you don't like your boss, you can honor his placement over your life and serve under him with a loyal spirit.

If God plants you in a ministry, then serve with an excellent spirit. God expected Korah to be faithful to Aaron—not because of anything Aaron had done—but because God had placed Aaron over Korah. When Korah dishonored that placement the consequences were disastrous.

When God sovereignly places you under someone's ministry for a season, your loyalty may be more to the office than to the man or woman. Even if the leader doesn't have the heart of David, the leader holds the office of David. God caused Aaron's rod to bud to demonstrate His loyalty to the office Aaron held. He will still cause the rod of leaders to blossom when they are in their God-appointed office. In other words, He will bless their ministry with His anointing. It's His imprimatur upon the office the person obediently holds.

Sometimes, we may find ourselves under a leader toward whom we struggle to feel loyal, and yet we know God has placed us there for

[10] Proverbs 17:6.
[11] Proverbs 22:1.
[12] As did Paul in 1 Thessalonians 2:19-20.

this season. I'm not saying, in such cases, that you must *feel* loyal to that leader; I am simply saying you should relate to that leader with a loyal spirit. That is, do nothing that could in any way be interpreted as treacherous. Do not spread slander or gossip; refuse to stir dissension; do not collect a group that has similar questions about the leader. Support the leader with integrity for as long as you are there. Do not leave with your mouth flapping. If God releases you to leave, leave quietly. *A loyal spirit has two options: relate to the leader with a noble spirit or leave quietly.*

Although David didn't trust Saul, he related to him with a loyal spirit. Even when he had opportunity, he refused to harm King Saul. He said, "'The LORD forbid that I should do this thing to my master, the LORD'S anointed, to stretch out my hand against him, seeing he is the anointed of the LORD'" (1 Samuel 24:6). As long as Saul was over him, David saw it as God's job to correct or discipline or remove Saul. It was his job to honor Saul. So even when David didn't feel loyal to Saul, he was loyal to Saul's office.

### Summation

When loyalty is built upon the right foundation, it has the potential not only to endure but to produce a tremendous spiritual harvest. In summary, then, here are some questions you might ask when trying to decide who to be loyal to.

- Does this David lay down his life for the sheep?
- Do I like where this David is going, and how he's getting there?
- Is this David loyal to God?
- Is God loyal to this David? Does God fight for him?
- Do I want to share in the promises given to this David?
- Is this David first a pursuer of God and second a servant of man?
- Is this David loyal to his friends?
- Is this David realistic and honest about his own weaknesses? Does insecurity rob him of a realistic self-assessment?
- Is this David's ambition to know God, or to grow a kingdom?
- Do I share a DNA compatibility with this David?
- Has God led me to submit myself to this David's leadership?

*For Group Discussion*

1.  Who are the mothers and fathers in Christ to whom you are loyal because of the history you share with them? Tell the group about one of them.

2.  Do you agree with the author, that a senior ministry leader has the right to desire loyalty from those who are paid staff?

3.  How does a person determine whether God is loyal to a certain leader?

4.  If it's unwise to express a *covenant* of loyalty to a local church, how should members express their *commitment*? Personalize this question for your church.

6.  What struck you most about Lot's story and his disloyalty to the man who had the promises?

7.  Is there anyone to whom you feel you've been a true spiritual son or daughter? A true spiritual father or mother?

8.  Discuss "loyalty to the office." Was there ever a time when you were loyal to the office or position a man or woman held, even when you didn't feel loyal to the person?

# CHAPTER 16

## *Commitment Versus Loyalty*

A sister once said to me, "Loyalty is commitment, isn't it?" My answer was, "No, loyalty and commitment are quite distinct from each other. Commitment has to do with faithfulness, whereas loyalty has to do with love."

It's quite easy to be committed to someone without being loyal to that person. Commitment is a function of the will that springs from the fountainhead of an excellent spirit. *A servant can be committed to you and faithful to all his responsibilities without actually being loyal to you.* That's not a negative thing; it's just an honest reality.

If you're the leader of a team, it's quite normative to expect commitment from every team member. You expect them to be faithful to their responsibilities, to be physically present at certain places and times, to be true to their word, dependable, punctual, and standing at their post when duty calls. You may even have a list of expectations that each member embraces before joining the team. To expect this level of commitment is totally reasonable because it is essential for team-building.

You cannot, however, expect your team members to be loyal to you. *Commitment can be required, loyalty cannot.* It's the difference between faithfulness and love.

While everyone on your team may be committed and faithful to the cause, not everyone truly loves. So if you're the leader of a team, chances are pretty good that not everyone on your team is loyal to you. That's not a bad or a wrong thing, nor should we be critical of those who don't have it; it's just something to be aware of. For team members to become loyal to their leader, God must do something sovereign in their hearts. *Either God gives them loyalty or they don't have it. Loyalty is the product of God's grace imparting love to the human spirit.*

The distinction between commitment and loyalty is important, but is not always fully understood. Some team leaders are taken by surprise, for example, when disloyalty arises from among some of their most committed members. The wise leader knows that just because someone is committed to the team does not guarantee that that person is loyal to the leader.

I say it this way to team leaders: *Require commitment, and promote loyalty.* You can ask people to be faithful, but you can't ask them to be loyal. For loyalty to be pure, it must by definition be voluntary. When you see loyalty being voluntarily evidenced by someone in your team, mark that person. You will be safe in giving him or her greater authority and responsibility in the team (provided that other qualities like faithfulness and humility are also present).

I'm not saying that we shouldn't reward those who are committed to the team faithfully, for it's scriptural to do so.[1] But you will be safest in giving the highest entrustments to those who are loyal.

*Commitment may be for a season, but loyalty is often for life.*

If you perceive that one of your team members is not yet loyal to you, do not allow yourself to be critical or offish toward that person lest you damage a relationship that has potential to progress.

Now a word to team members: Be cautious around a leader who requires loyalty. Wise leaders will watch for and honor loyalty, but they cannot require or demand it. *Anyone who requires loyalty doesn't really understand it and is using the requirement as a smokescreen to mask their insecurities.* The compassionate leader gives time for the weak members on the team to grow in loyalty. Some team members may still be working through emotional baggage from loyalties that were violated ten or twenty years ago.

If you don't feel loyal toward the one who is over you in the Lord, that does not necessarily mean there is something wrong with you. It may mean that loyalty will take time to develop. *The Lord will not require you to feel loyal to every leader in your life; but He certainly will*

---

[1] Luke 16:10.

*require you to show commitment to your leaders.*

Walk in commitment and love, and see if the Lord gives you loyalty over time.

Let me point to one more dynamic that distinguishes commitment from loyalty. Suppose there has been a breach of relationship and now you're trying to repair the damage. If the breach happened with someone who was committed to you, it's possible to restore that person to his previous commitment levels by apologizing and reaching out in tenderness and love. However, if the breach has happened with someone who was loyal to you, but he feels his loyalty was violated or spurned, it is much more difficult to restore that hurt person back to loyalty. For loyalty to be restored requires supernatural intervention. Commitment can be restored with effort—but loyalty? It's rare indeed. This is one reason why the Bible allows for divorce in cases of sexual immorality.[2] Once the fidelity of the marital covenant has been violated, God Himself recognizes the difficulty of repairing it.

### When Loyalty Is Lost, Is It Beyond Recovery?

We have just said that it is rare for loyalty, once lost, to be restored. This goes along with Proverbs 18:19, "A brother offended is harder to win than a strong city." And yet it is not always beyond recovery.

We'll glean greater insight into this principle by looking at the examples of Jesus' disciples, Judas Iscariot and Peter. Both Judas and Simon Peter suffered a collapse in their loyalty to Jesus. But the nature of their crisis was different, and it landed them in two totally different places. The loyalty of one was restored, that of the other was not.

Peter denied the Lord three times, even with oaths, which was certainly an act of disloyalty. Judas betrayed Jesus to the arresting soldiers, and that too was an act of disloyalty. But Peter did not suffer Judas's fate. Judas suffered eternal damnation for his disloyalty, and Peter suffered only a sifting process that actually turned him into a better man. What was different about their respective disloyalties?

The answer is in this: *Peter's disloyalty was rooted in a loss of faith; Judas's disloyalty was rooted in a loss of love.*

Let me remind you of our working definition of loyalty, which

---

[2] Matthew 19:9.

states that loyalty involves both faith and love:

> Loyalty is a noble, unswerving allegiance, rooted in faith and love, that binds hearts together in common purpose.

Peter had a faith crisis. When Jesus was arrested, his confidence that Jesus would emerge victoriously suddenly collapsed. Because of Jesus' intercession, Peter's faith did not fail completely.[3] But it came close. He almost lost it. He lost enough of his faith that he denied he even knew the Lord. But even though his faith crumpled, he never lost his love. He wormed his way into Jesus' trial because of love. Later, when Jesus asked him, "Do you love Me?" Peter was so passionate in asserting his love.[4] "Jesus, You know I love You," he cried. "I've always loved You. I never lost my love for You." Peter's crisis was a loss of faith, not of love.

Not so with Judas. In his case, Judas Iscariot lost his love. It happened over time, no doubt, and was finally clinched on the day that Jesus rebuked him. Judas thought that Mary's extravagance in pouring the expensive ointment all over Jesus was wasteful. But Jesus rebuked Judas for hassling her. "'Let her alone,'" He said to Judas.[5]

Judas looked at Jesus and realized he no longer loved this Man. He actually despised Him. It was at that moment he turned on his heels, went to the chief priests, and agreed to find a way to betray Jesus to them. When Judas became disloyal because of a love loss, nothing could turn him back. Even his remorse after the betrayal could not lead him to godly repentance. When he lost his love, his loyalty was forever gone.

In the cases of Judas and Peter, their breakdown regarded their loyalty to the Lord. But the same principles hold true as regards loyalty to God's Davids. When believers lose their loyalty to one of God's leaders because of a *faith crisis*—because they struggle to believe that God is still fighting for this David—that loss of loyalty has the potential to be turned around. But when they lose their loyalty because of a *love loss*, how can it be retrieved?

The same dynamic can be seen in Job's life. When Job went

---

[3] Luke 22:32.
[4] See John 21:15-19.
[5] Mark 14:6.

through his ordeal, his friends became disloyal to him, but it was because they lost faith in his position with God, not because they lost their love. They actually loved Job right through the whole confrontation. They just didn't believe that God's favor was upon him. Because it was a faith crisis and not a love crisis, they were able to be restored to Job at the end of the book.[6]

The same thing happened to the eleven disciples. They all fled from Jesus in fear because their faith collapsed. But since their love for Jesus carried their hearts, they were later reunited to Him in affectionate allegiance.

If you have a loyalty loss toward your leader because of a *faith crisis*—that is, because you doubt whether God is truly standing with him or her, then slow down. Don't pass judgment prematurely. Watch and wait. Time may prove you were wrong, and God may truly vindicate His David in your eyes. If that happens, the Lord can change your heart and renew the loyalty that was once estranged.

But if your loyalty loss is due to a *love crisis*—that is, because you have lost your respect and come to despise the leader whom you once honored, what can be done about that kind of breach? Can that kind of love loss be repaired and the previous loyalty restored? In Judas's case, the answer was "no."

### *Extravagant Loyalty Triggers Disloyalty*

While we're considering Judas and the factors that led to Christ's crucifixion, I would like to show—especially for the praise and worship leaders reading this book—how it was that extravagant praise and worship (which are expressions of loving loyalty) contributed to Christ's crucifixion. (Pardon me while we chase down this bunnytrail.)

First of all, it was extravagant praise that triggered the envy of the chief priests. When they saw the multitudes praising Jesus with abandoned joy at His triumphal entry into Jerusalem, it was like the proverbial straw that broke the camel's back. "The Pharisees therefore said among themselves, 'You see that you are accomplishing nothing. Look, the world has gone after Him!'" (John 12:19). That effusion of praise—with palm branches and cries of "Hosanna!"—brought their

[6] See Job 42:7-10.

envy to the boiling point because of Jesus' popularity. The extravagant praises of the masses sealed the resolve of the Pharisees to crucify Jesus.

At the same time, extravagant worship was at work to precipitate Christ's death. I'm referring here to the supper in Bethany when Mary opened the expensive jar of perfume and poured its entire contents upon the Lord. That Jesus would affirm this waste was more than Judas could handle. This effusion of worship was more than just a token of love; it was a gripping demonstration of loyalty. When Judas Iscariot saw the extravagance of Mary's loyalty to Christ, it pushed him over the edge. That is, as he gazed upon her loyalty, he was forced to look at the disloyalty of his own heart. Her zeal was revealing all the hesitation in his own spirit. He had two ways to respond. Either he could look at his own heart in straightforward honesty and do business with God, or he could justify his responses. He chose the latter, hardened his heart, and went out to plot the betrayal.

*It was Mary's lavish loyalty that triggered Judas' disloyalty, which in turn precipitated Jesus' crucifixion.* There are times when one person's affectionate allegiance will force everyone else on the team to play their hand.

By loving Jesus extravagantly, Mary was putting forces into motion much greater than she ever realized. Her loyalty was actually going to get Jesus killed. In a similar way, it is extravagant praise and worship that will be the catalysts for the consummation of all things in these last days. The Pharisees will be mobilized by their offence at extravagant, public displays of praise, and will try to stop the rivers of revival; and the Judases, offended by the lavish expressions of lovesick, loyal worshipers at the end of the age, will rise up in disloyalty against God's Davids.

But as offences proliferate, loving loyalty will be restored simultaneously in the earth. The return of Christ will be heralded by the greatest resurgence of affectionate allegiance the world has ever seen.

### For Group Discussion

1. Do you agree with the author's distinction between loyalty and commitment? What commitments are required of your team members? Have you ever had a time when your commitment naturally evolved into loyalty?

2. Have you ever known someone who was both committed and disloyal at the same time?

3. "Require commitment, and promote loyalty"—do you consider that a good rule of thumb?

4. Talk about the similarities and differences you see between Peter's and Judas's disloyalty.

5. "By loving Jesus extravagantly, Mary was putting forces into motion much greater than she ever realized. Her loyalty was actually going to get Jesus killed." Talk about that. Have you ever considered that the extravagance of your praise and worship might have the potential to reveal someone else's disloyalty? What's going on in people's hearts when they're irritated by someone else's praise or worship?

# CHAPTER 17

# *Rewards Of Loyalty*

*L*oyalty hasn't always gotten real positive press in the body of Christ. But I want to do my part to turn the tide. It's time to sing its praises. Today's generation needs to know the value of loyalty so that they can pursue it with pure hearts. I'm blatant about it—my goal is to entice you to loyalty.

I have sprinkled loyalty's praises throughout this book, but now I want to concentrate on some of the rewards of loyalty. My prayer is that you'll come away from this book with a holy covetousness—a desire for a loyal spirit to both God and David.

### Those Loyal to David Enjoy the Blessings of David's Enrichment

The nation of Israel was never as rich and prosperous as in the days of David and Solomon, when loyalty was at its zenith. God blessed David because He was in covenant with David,[1] and the entire nation was consequently blessed because they stood with David. When God enriches David, David shares the blessing with all. He doesn't serve for his own enrichment but for the enrichment of the nation.

Here's how God helped David: Invading armies were repulsed; the hemorrhage caused by marauding raiders was stopped; and vast spoils of war suddenly poured into the kingdom because of substantial conquests. Under David, the entire nation experienced a tremendous acceleration of enrichment.

---

[1] See 2 Chronicles 7:10.

The most blessed saints in the land today are those who are standing in loyalty with their David. You will never regret loyalty given in faith and love to God's Davids. *When David is enriched, you too will be enriched.*

In practical terms within the local church, this enrichment typically translates into benefits such as increased ministry opportunities, more people to serve, a geographically wider sphere of influence, better facilities, more spiritual momentum, and a greater supply of resources (people resources, literary resources, training resources, financial resources, etc.). All of these benefits combine to provide greater opportunity for enduring Kingdom fruitfulness.

### Loyal People Are A Delight To Lead

*When people are loyal to you in love, you will find great pleasure in leading them forward in your Kingdom mandates.* With those who are not loyal, you are likely to find yourself constantly hitting little snags as you journey together, necessitating conflict resolution. Where loyalty is lacking, relational cleanup and conflict resolution require a lot more work (time and energy). Sometimes the sheer volume of words necessary to resolve tensions with people who aren't loyal is tiresome and tedious. *Where loyalty is present, conflict resolution is so much easier on the leaders.* Misunderstandings are cleared up with incredible ease when relationships are lubricated with affectionate allegiance. This is why we are counseled, "Obey those who rule over you, and be submissive, for they watch out for your souls, as those who must give account. Let them do so with joy and not with grief, for that would be unprofitable for you" (Hebrews 13:17). It is to everyone's advantage when David finds it a joy to lead the people.

*When a team is loyal to their leader, they are much more eager to go with their leader's initiatives.* They trust the leader's motives and ability to hear from God, so when the leader says, "I believe I have an idea from the Lord," his team answers with a willing spirit. The team will certainly give feedback and perspective, fine-tuning the idea with wisdom, and at times even talking the leader out of his idea. But their first response is to be optimistic rather than hitting the brakes because their desire is to move forward together in Kingdom exploits. This is the kind of team that every leader wants to lead! In contrast, where loyalty has deteriorated or been damaged, a leader can hear an audible voice from heaven and his followers will still be resistant. The burden of leading in that kind of context is unprofitable for everyone.

Some people's spirits are only managed by information. When the Lord has not given them loyalty of heart, they will be inclined to question your motives more frequently than those who are loyal. The only way they are placated is when they are assured, through much information, that your motives are noble. Once they've been given all the information, they can relax and join you in the project. But the process will need to be repeated again and again with each new endeavor. Leading these kinds of people requires extra energy, is wearisome, and dampens the leader's joy.

Loyal people, in contrast, have an eager spirit and are ready at a moment's notice to run with you to battle. What a joy!

If one of your team members is uncertain about how safe you are as a leader, they will often analyze every move you make. They will analyze your decisions, your motives, your thought processes, and your logic. They will analyze you, not because they want to know you, but because they want to know how to maneuver around you. This is how Satan relates to God. He is constantly analyzing God, not because he wants to know God, but because he's always trying to figure God out. Satan is always trying to get inside God's head, trying to read His game plan, wanting to anticipate His next move, trying to deduce where God is going with the thing.

In contrast, those who are loyal to God in love want to come into relationship with Him. They want to know all the same information, but for a very different reason. They want to know what He's thinking because every revelation of the mind of Christ causes them to bow in renewed affection and awe. They want to know His plans and purposes because it will empower them to run at His side as He goes forth into His harvest.

Similarly, those who are loyal to David need communication and information, but it's all for the purpose of enabling them to serve alongside David with maximum impact.

*Ah, loyalty makes the relationship a delightful adventure of mutual discovery.*

## *Loyalty Multiplies Ministry Effectiveness*

When a team joins hands together in loyalty and unity, that team is able to do greater exploits together than if all the team members were scattered and doing their own thing. The total impact is greater than the sum of the parts. Loyalty binds hearts together for common purpose in the Kingdom, multiplying the effectiveness of the Gospel.

God gave to David a sphere of tens of thousands, and then David surrounded himself with leaders who each had a sphere of thousands.[2] When the leaders of thousands come under the leadership of David, they find their greatest success and breadth of ministry impact. And at the same time, David enters into the fullness of his destiny. The Davidic dynasty enjoyed such glory and eminence because the captains all came together in loyalty to serve David.

The same still holds true today. As long as the leaders of thousands are scattered abroad in individual pursuits, the fullness of the Kingdom will not be realized. But when the captains and princes in Israel join together in loyalty under God's Davids, something explosive will happen within the church of Jesus Christ. The Kingdom of God will be manifest in our midst in Davidic glory. Where this principle is being understood today, we are seeing massive ministries being raised up in the earth that are numbered, not by thousands of people, but by tens of thousands and, yes, even hundreds of thousands. It's a phenomenon unparalleled in church history. And in every instance, loyalty to the David of the house is clearly established.

It is better, in my judgment, to hazard the risks of loyalty and give our hearts to God's Davids, than to hold ourselves at a distance for fear we might be disappointed or hurt.

I travel to quite a few churches in the USA and abroad, and I have noticed a pattern that holds consistently true: *The churches with the greatest impact in their region are those that have a strong loyalty to their David, their senior leader.* It is unmistakable—there is a clear link between loyalty and compounded ministry effectiveness.

## *Loyalty Weathers Storms Better*

Storms are inevitable in the body of Christ. We will hit seasons

[2] 2 Samuel 18:1.

of struggle, accusation, reproach, rumors, conflict, hardship, etc. It's only when the storm comes that the strength of our infrastructures are proven and manifest. Will the team collapse? Will the ministry utterly fall?

Loyalty is like "Liquid Nails." It's the glue that will keep a team together through the tough times. It's loyalty to David (the team leader) that will enable the team to survive the turbulence and come through intact. *When the primary leadership around a leader is loyal, they are able to love the leader through the misunderstandings, through the questions, through the times of uncertainty, and persevere through to the calmer waters of consensus and shared vision. When a team is loyal to its leader in this way, the times of difficulty have the least adverse affect upon the congregation.* Loyalty will save the congregation from undue trauma and hurt and will keep it from becoming unnecessarily dispersed across the countryside in the wake of the storm. Blessed are the people whose leaders are loyal to their David. When the storm hits, that leadership team will hold together in affectionate allegiance, and any damage to the congregation will be minimized.

*Loyalty preserves the weak ones in the midst.* When storms move through, the strong believers usually survive. The ones who are typically the spiritual casualties are the weak ones, the babes in Christ. When there is a breach in the leadership, the weak ones are those most easily offended, or turned aside, or most easily drawn away under the influence of leaders with self-seeking motives. Loyalty helps to repair the breach, which in turn preserves the weak ones from having to deal with matters too weighty for them.

In contrast, where disloyalty finds a footing, there can be a groundswell against David fueled by discontented leaders who trumpet their personal convictions under the banner of "speaking the truth." This kind of relational hotbed has the potential to erupt and damage many in the flock. Sadly, this happens much too often in the body of Christ.

I realize, of course, that some leaders do not have the heart of David, but are guilty of falling into error or repressive leadership methods, bringing due reproach upon themselves. But we are speaking here of the true Davids of God. *When the storm hits a team where a David is at the helm, loyalty will cement the foundations of that team, and they will survive the storm with the least amount of collateral damage.*

### *Loyalty Has Its Own Boast*

When Paul appealed to the Corinthians for their loyalty, he wrote, "we are your boast as you also are ours, in the day of the Lord Jesus" (2 Corinthians 1:14). In the day of Christ, Paul would boast that the Corinthians were among the fruits of his labors; and the Corinthians would boast that Paul was their beloved apostolic leader.

The loyal spirit will have a boast on the day of Jesus Christ: "I was loyal to this servant of Christ, and behold, he or she is now honored of God as a true servant of the Lord. I was loyal in the midst of persecution and resistance, in the midst of controversy, in the midst of accusation and misunderstanding, in the midst of trial and perplexity. I was loyal to one of God's Davids."

And the servant of the Lord will boast: "I was loyal to these saints, I poured my life out for them, and now here they stand, presented perfect before the throne of God without fault and with great glory."

Not everyone at Corinth remained loyal to Paul. But imagine the joy of those saints in Corinth who will stand at the last day and say to Jesus, "I was loyal to Paul in love, even when it wasn't popular in Corinth to be so. This great apostle who now stands at Your right hand, exonerated from all accusation, whose writings have changed the course of history—I did not cast aside my loyalty to this great David. By grace alone, the loyalty of Christ sustained my heart, and now I boast in this grace of God."

### *God Rewards Loyalty With A Posterity*

Jeremiah tells the most fascinating story of how the Lord told him to call the family of the Rechabites into the house of the Lord and offer them wine to drink.[3] They refused, replying to Jeremiah, "'We will drink no wine, for Jonadab the son of Rechab, our father, commanded us, saying, "You shall drink no wine, you nor your sons, forever"'" (Jeremiah 35:6).

The Lord used this as a living parable to say to the people of Israel, in so many words, "The sons of Jonadab have been loyal to their father for several generations, refusing to drink wine because their father so commanded them. But you, the people of Israel, have not been loyal

---

[3] See Jeremiah 35.

to Me, to obey My commandments. The sons of Jonadab have been more loyal to their natural father than you have been to your heavenly Father."

As a result, God pronounced a judgment against the nation.[4] The loyalty of the Rechabites became a righteous witness against the people of Israel, incurring judgment upon the people.[5]

And what happened to the Rechabite clan? God's promise to them was powerful:

> And Jeremiah said to the house of the Rechabites, "Thus says the LORD of hosts, the God of Israel: 'Because you have obeyed the commandment of Jonadab your father, and kept all his precepts and done according to all that he commanded you, therefore thus says the LORD of hosts, the God of Israel: "Jonadab the son of Rechab shall not lack a man to stand before Me forever"'" (Jeremiah 35:18-19).

Right now, as you read these words, there are Jews alive on the earth who are the direct descendants of Jonadab. Until the day that Jesus returns, Jonadab will have Jewish offspring in the earth. Wow— what an assurance! This family has been guaranteed a living posterity in the presence of God—all because of their loyalty.

Such a compelling promise only serves to strengthen our confidence in this truth: God loves loyalty and rewards it with His favor.

### Mordecai's Reward

A reader might complain, "I've been loyal for years, but I've not seen it produce any favor in my life to this point. Sometimes I'm not even sure if my leader knows I exist." Well, let me encourage you with the example of Morcedai.

Mordecai was an upright man in the Bible who learned that two of the king's eunuchs were plotting, out of anger, to murder the king. Mordecai immediately sent a warning to the king. The king checked out Mordecai's story, and when it was corroborated. he killed the two eunuchs who had concocted the treasonous plan. But then the king did nothing to recognize Mordecai's loyalty or thank him for his kindness.

---

[4] See Jeremiah 35:17.
[5] Compare 2 Corinthians 2:16.

Mordecai could have become cynical and said, "What's the point of being loyal to the king? It's gotten me nowhere. This king has no appreciation for those who support him!" However, he chose to guard his heart and to simply continue serving the king.

What Mordecai didn't know was that his kindness had been recorded in the king's archives. It was a kindness that was recorded on earth and was in Mordecai's "assets account" in heaven. The time came when God decided to cash in Mordecai's assets. God simply gave the king a sleepless night; the king decided he wanted someone to read to him; and the thing that was read to him was the record of how Mordecai had been loyal to him by exposing the assassination plot.

When the king was reminded of Mordecai's allegiance, he realized he had never shown his gratitude. So he took specific steps that day to honor Mordecai. A royal robe was placed upon Mordecai; he was seated upon the king's horse; then a powerful prince named Haman paraded him through the streets of the capital city and shouted accolades before him.

The point of this story is that even though loyalty may not seem to be rewarded at the time, it is nevertheless noted in heaven. And one day God can call up that which you've invested in your "assets account" and reward you to the full.

By the time the whole story was written, Mordecai ended up being seated at the right hand of the king and administrating the affairs of the entire kingdom. Take a cue from Mordecai's loyalty. Who knows what kinds of promotion God has in store for you as you are loyal to those God has placed over you in the Lord?

### Another Loyalty Story

I want to end this chapter with a story about one of my personal friends, Bill, who serves as worship pastor in a prominent church in Virginia. He told me how he was on staff at this church, but then through a series of awkward circumstances and some disappointments left that church for another staff position in another state. A couple years later, the pastor of his former church called and asked if he would be willing to come back to Virginia and interview for a different staff position in their church. When Bill returned for a visit and spoke with the pastor about the possibility of returning to this church that he had once left, the pastor said to him, "Do you know why you're here? It's because, after you left the first time, I never heard a peep." The pastor was expecting to incur some negative backlash for the way he had handled Bill and encouraged him to leave. But Bill didn't spread any rancor to anyone in the church; he just left quietly. The pastor said to him, "I knew that was a difficult period for you, and yet you didn't spread any slander in the body. You were loyal to me." It was because of that loyalty that the pastor asked him to return. Bill was hired a second time, and today is enjoying a very fruitful ministry on the staff of this vibrant church with a regional impact. This true story is inspiring because Bill guarded his loyalty to the pastor, and the pastor was wise enough to recognize and reward that loyalty.

### For Group Discussion

1. What link do you see between the incredible affluence the nation enjoyed under David's rule and the fact that the people were exceptionally loyal to David?

2. Have you experienced the contrast of leading some who were loyal, and others who weren't? Did you discover how difficult it was to resolve conflicts among those who lacked loyalty? Tell the group your story.

3. Do you agree with the author's opinion that the churches with the greatest ministry impact are usually strongest in loyalty to their leader?

4. What have you noticed happens to the weak members of the body when disloyalty brings separation among brethren?

5. Read Jeremiah 35. How does this story of the Rechabites speak to you personally, and to your team?

# CHAPTER 18

# *Loyalty To David Will Be Tested*

With the rewards of loyalty being so rich, it's impossible to gain ground in this territory without it being contested. Satan will attack us in order to undermine our loyalty, and God will test us in order to purify and strengthen our loyalty.

We never really know for sure if loyalty is genuine until it's proven. You can think you have it in your team, but wait until a storm hits. Adversity often surprises us in what it reveals. Some we thought were not are revealed to be loyal, while others we thought were loyal will turn away. *Loyalty shines best when challenged most.*

Adversity proves not only our loyalty to God, but also our loyalty to David. If people turned away from Jesus, who handled them perfectly, should we be shocked if people turn away from God's Davids who handle people imperfectly? If Jesus was easy to get offended at, how much more God's Davids? Yes, loyalty to David will be tested. To remain standing in loyalty to David can be one of the greatest challenges of the Christian walk because sometimes he or she is infuriatingly human.

Loyalty to David can be faked—but only for so long. Eventually, something will happen to test loyalty. It's inevitable. If your loyalty to David isn't authentic, it's only a matter of time before the truth surfaces.

Disloyalty will not remain hidden forever. Eventually true colors will surface. This is why Paul, in listing qualifications for deacons, instructed that they first be "proved" for a season.[1] What is it that is being proved? The deacon's maturity. "Not a novice, lest being puffed up with pride he fall into the same condemnation as the devil" (1 Timothy 3:6). When pride rises in a novice, he is tempted with the same treachery that condemned the devil. Anyone can pretend loyalty temporarily; but a protracted testing season is in order before appointing deacons so that loyalty can be proven. Once proven, a deacon is qualified for the privilege of serving the saints, thus obtaining "a good standing and great boldness in the faith which is in Christ Jesus" (1 Timothy 3:13).

Paul spoke of how Timothy had proven his loyalty: "But you know his proven character, that as a son with his father he served with me in the gospel" (Philippians 2:22). Timothy proved, over time, that he was a true son. Paul further said, "For I have no one like-minded, who will sincerely care for your state. For all seek their own, not the things which are of Christ Jesus" (Philippians 2:20-21). Paul is speaking of leaders who were more loyal to themselves than they were to Christ. Because Timothy was loyal to Christ (v. 21), he was able to be loyal to Paul (v. 22). *Only as the sons are emptied of their own kingdom-building inclinations will they be able to sustain loyalty toward the spiritual fathers.* What was Timothy's reward for his loyalty? Paul entrusted him with greater spiritual responsibility.[2] When Paul said Timothy's loyalty was "proven," he meant that Timothy had ample opportunity to develop a negative attitude toward Paul and forsake him. He lived in close enough proximity to see all of Paul's shortcomings. He wasn't always handled perfectly. But Timothy loved. He loved Paul. He remained true. So Timothy goes down in Bible history as one of the ultimate examples of true, godly loyalty.

Loyalty must be based on something other than David's performance and leadership skills. Otherwise, it won't go the distance. It must be based on the confidence that God is loyal to this David, even though he is imperfect. *A loyal spirit recognizes that God is with David, warts and all.* The man who can preserve his loyalty to David, even after seeing his mistakes, will share in a dimension of fruitfulness that those who become offended will not taste.

*In some cases, disloyalty has a valid grievance.* For example, I'm sure that David didn't handle Absalom absolutely perfectly. In other cases,

---

[1] 1 Timothy 3:10, KJV.
[2] See Philippians 2:19.

it doesn't have a valid grievance. I'm thinking of Judas who betrayed Jesus, even though Jesus had handled him perfectly. The point is not whether your grievance is valid or not; the point is that you've allowed your heart to become offended with God's David. If you stay in that place of offence, you'll lose. *One of the trademarks of loyalty is its commitment to process grievances properly and emerge from the thing still on David's team.* Those who weather the grievance and still prove their loyalty are "true sons."

When you're serving under a David, you're going to encounter increased spiritual attacks, because David attracts warfare. The enemy is after him, and one of the enemy's primary ways of getting at David is by stirring dissension in the ranks of his sons. So if you're one of David's sons, you had better place a guard around your heart lest you succumb to Satan's schemes. Satan wants to get you offended with David. You'll be under attack at times when you're not even aware of it. There are times you'll think your opinion is so justifiable, when in fact you're being tantalized with disloyalty.

God has so many fascinating ways to reveal the true nature of our loyalty. I remember once taking a couple brothers with me on a ministry trip. I sincerely thought these men were totally loyal to me. I had been invited to come and speak, and my hosts had agreed to provide for my prayer partners to come with me, so I asked these brothers to come. But after we got to the ministry setting, and I was given a larger platform for ministry than they, their insecurities surfaced, and they became unsettled. They were uncomfortable with what they perceived to be the magnification of one vessel's ministry (mine) rather than an equal sharing of ministry by all on the team. They didn't realize it, but God was allowing their loyalty to be tested. They seemed to think that I was being unduly exalted, whereas from my perspective I was simply fulfilling the speaking ministry my hosts were asking of me. They had known me on our "home turf," but when they saw how I was honored on another ministry field, they became disturbed. I thought the brothers were loyal to me, but was surprised at what surfaced when the right set of circumstances arose. *That's the way of loyalty; its genuineness is not known until certain conditions give it the occasion to be proven.*

### Ways Our Loyalty To David Is Proved

I see at least five common ways in which our loyalty to one of God's Davids might be proved.

## 1. Loyalty to David is proved when David makes a mistake.

Sometimes David is downright wrong. I can promise you this: Stick with David long enough and he will eventually fall short of your expectations. That statement is true about every human leader. David will never purposely disappoint you because he has the heart of a true shepherd. But he's still human, and despite his best intentions he will disappoint.

If David had handled everything perfectly, it would have been a lot easier to be loyal to him. It was his mistakes and shortcomings that convinced his antagonists of the justification of their cause.

Joab, David's army commander, is a sad example of a man who couldn't get past his offence toward David. David had made some mistakes with Joab. Still, Joab stood faithfully for many years, straight through Absalom's uprising. But near the end of David's lifetime, Joab turned and joined in Adonijah's insurrection. Joab ran most of the race with David, but then at ten minutes to midnight he lost it. He became disloyal just as the race was coming to a close. Why? Because David had rebuked him a couple times and mishandled him a couple times, and Joab was unwilling to forgive David for the wrong and claim ownership for his own failures. Bitterness eventually overtook his heart and he turned from David.

The issue is not simply how long you have run or how well you have run, but how you have finished. Joab ran most of his race well, but then crashed near the finish line. Disloyalty derailed him.

Loyalty must see past the humanity of the leader. "'Love will cover a multitude of sins'" (1 Peter 4:8). Loyalty (because it loves) has this ability to cover the sins of the leader and still continue to walk together. *Love is the power that carries loyalty to the finish line.*

## 2. Loyalty to David is proved when God crushes David.

Sometimes God crushes David as part of the formative process of making him a great leader. When David is being crucified, it challenges all the loyalties of those on his team. While enduring the cross, David cannot provide for his sons what he once could. He's not able to feed or to lead as he once did. Some people will give their loyalty to a certain leader because of that leader's ability to lead the charge. *Loyalty based on the leader's reputation or ability to perform is frail indeed.* It's a ticking time bomb—especially if God plans a crucifixion for that leader. That's why loyalty to David should be based upon God's promises to him rather than upon his ministry giftings.

When David is crucified, it looks like God has abandoned him. If David's sons don't have a "cross paradigm," they will see David's pain and conclude that God is against him. This is what happened to Job's friends; because they had no cross paradigm (an understanding of how God crucifies His Davids for Kingdom purpose), they became disloyal to God's man.

At the end of his life, Paul uttered these sad words, "At my first defense no one stood with me, but all forsook me. May it not be charged against them" (2 Timothy 4:16). These words are reminiscent of Gethsemane. Paul had drunk so deeply of the sufferings of Christ that, at the end of his life, it appeared to his associates that he had been abandoned by God. Wrongly discerning Paul's status with God, they abandoned their loyalty for Paul in favor of more promising pursuits. But Paul was the man with promises who was helped by his God, and they were very unwise to forsake him this late in the race.

It happened with David, with Paul, and with Jesus. When Jesus was crucified, the loyalties of the disciples were tested to their fullest. The disciples had a measure of faith in Jesus, but they didn't have enough to believe in Him when He was struck by God and crushed. They lost faith in the promises they thought were given to Jesus. In the hour of proving, they forsook Jesus in the garden and left Him alone. By the way, it's fascinating to note that the women who followed Jesus remained at His side faithfully to the end. Could that possibly be one reason why Jesus appeared first to a woman after His resurrection?

As the Bible stories indicate, there are few who are able to remain loyal to David through the crushing.

## 3. Loyalty to David is proved when there are differences of judgment.

As we have said, loyalty doesn't mean you never disagree with David. But it does mean you're careful how and where you express your disagreement.

*Loyalty defers in judgment.* What is a judgment? Simply put, a judgment is a coming to a final decision.

A judgment is stronger than an opinion. Judgment says, "I've looked at all the evidence; I've heard the arguments from all sides; I've given studied consideration to all the implications; and now I'm rendering judgment."

Opinions are generally held more loosely and can be swayed or changed if more compelling arguments are presented. Judgment, however, carries with it the implication that all arguments have been heard, weighed thoughtfully, and now a final decision has been made. Judgment is usually beyond negotiation. Judgment has heard the wisdom of the elders, it has looked at life's experiences, and it has formulated its verdict on the matter.

When David passes judgment on certain matters, it's no longer up for discussion; a decision is made. At that moment, loyalty is often tested. But loyalty will remain true to David, even if it disagrees with David's decision. Because loyalty runs deeper than individual decisions. It seeks to "be perfectly joined together in the same mind and in the same judgment" with David (1 Corinthians 1:10).

For example, when David insisted on counting the armies of Israel, Joab did the right thing to eventually defer to David's judgment. He did his best to talk David out of it, but he knew that loyalty would require that he defer. It was right for Joab to express his opinion—even forcefully. But then it was also right for him to defer in loyalty to David's judgment when David was resolute. Even though David was wrong, Joab helped to enact the legislation because he believed that God was able to bring His leader to account.

When Barnabas could not submit to Paul's judgment regarding John Mark, it was evident Barnabas did not have the loyalty of a son toward Paul. That's not a criticism of Barnabas, but simply a truthful acknowledgement of the nature of their relationship.

When Apollos would not go to Corinth at Paul's behest, it was evidence that Apollos did not have the loyalty of a son toward Paul. That's not to say that Apollos was any less for it; it's just that Apollos was not a son to Paul. To be loyal to Paul as a true son would include deferring to Paul's judgment, but Apollos made his own judgment in the matter. When differences of judgment arose, then it became obvious where true loyalties lay.

## 4. Loyalty to David is proved when David hesitates to install or promote a leader.

David had good reason to hesitate in installing Solomon as king, but it was during the season of no movement that disloyalty was brewing. Adonijah used his father's hesitation to gather his forces and coalesce a conspiracy. *Disloyalty is quick to step into the seeming void of inactivity.*

Neither Absalom nor Adonijah could wait for David to give them their portion; they thought they had to take matters into their own hands. Solomon, in contrast, waited for his father to give him his inheritance. *Loyalty will wait.* Disloyalty demands immediate action, but loyalty waits patiently.

It's easy for sons to misunderstand fathers during the waiting period. To the son, it seems like the father is withholding. But the father has a vantage the son doesn't have. The thing that saves the relationship is loyalty. If the son is loyal, he will walk with the father through the season of withholding and discipline until he is given his inheritance. *The loyal son never tries to take what is rightfully his but always waits to receive it from the father.*

Few things are as controversial on a team as when the leader hesitates to promote a son or daughter who appears by everyone else to be a great candidate for promotion. Those who are disloyal will misread the leader and accuse him or her of being controlling, inflexible, overly suspicious, or unwilling to share authority. In a few cases, those accusations may be true—there are a few leaders out there who have a problem releasing areas of responsibility. But in most cases, the leader is probably hesitating in wisdom borne out of discernment, knowing that the son or daughter is not yet ready for promotion. In the process, however, everyone's loyalties are tested.

## 5. Loyalty to David is proved when David dismisses one of his leaders.

When David dismissed Joab from his position as commander of

the army and replaced him with Amasa, everything went crazy. Sheba, son of Bichri, capitalized upon the season of chaos and stirred up his own rebellion against David. And then Joab murdered Amasa. It was perhaps the most turbulent season in David's entire reign.[3]

One of the most disruptive things a pastor can do is dismiss an elder, or someone on the pastoral team, or someone in an influential place of leadership in the church. Large churches with multiple staff find this one of their greatest problem areas. Adding staff is rarely a problem; but when you have to release staff members from their jobs or ministries, be ready for troubled waters.

And here's why. Joab always has a circle of friends around him who are more loyal to him than they are to David. As long as Joab is in his place under David, his friends don't have to choose loyalties. To be loyal to Joab is to be loyal to David. But when Joab is removed, everyone suddenly has to choose between Joab and David. If Joab has any disloyalty working in him at all, he will be able to use the dismissal as an opportunity to collect his loyal friends around himself. He will decide that David is wrong, and so will feel justified in gathering a circle of friends who share in his offence.

As ministries or businesses grow and become large, it becomes inevitable that not everyone can have personal contact with David (the senior leader) directly. The only way David can lead is by delegating authority and responsibility to a circle of associates around himself. If the ministry is large enough, those associates in turn have their own networks of support personnel who implement the vision of the ministry. Large ministries have these kinds of concentric layers of connectedness surrounding the primary leader. This is wise leadership, but it inevitably means that some people will become more loyal to one of David's helpers than they are to David himself.

David is fully aware of this dynamic, but since he has settled his insecurities in the love of God, he releases responsibility freely to others. However, he realizes he is making himself vulnerable to his support team. He places in the hands of his associates the power to do him harm. It's the risk inherent in love. David loves his associates, so he freely releases responsibility to them without taking self-protective measures. If any one of them becomes disloyal and decides to spread

[3] See 2 Samuel 19-20.

slander against David, David will unavoidably suffer loss. At such times, the verse holds true, "There is a time in which one man rules over another to his own hurt" (Ecclesiastes 8:9).

*If we were not somehow making ourselves vulnerable to each other in love, loyalty would not be such a radiant jewel.* It's loyalty's risks that make it so precious. It is a rare treasure indeed when a ministry team functions together in undefiled loyalty over the course of many years.

When Joab is dismissed, there are two ways he can leave: He can galvanize all those who are loyal to him and draw them away; or he can shut his mouth and leave quietly, doing nothing to damage the loyalty of anyone else. Even if he is not loyal to the leader, this latter is the option chosen by the man with an excellent spirit and a noble heart.

To Joab (the staff member who is dismissed) and his loyalists, let me say this: Even if you have been violated by the leader of the house, remember that the way you leave this house is the way you'll enter the next house. *What you sow in the leaving process is what you will reap in the next place you land.* How you leave is intensely important to God. If you leave the right way, you can sow seeds of loyalty into your future.

### For Group Discussion

1. How have you noticed spiritual warfare to be more intense around God's Davids?
2. How has the Lord helped you to remain loyal when you've seen David's weaknesses?
3. How should we walk in our team when we have differences of judgment on how to proceed?
4. If David were to dismiss you from your position today, how would you respond?

# PART THREE
## *The Specter Of Disloyalty*

Those who fall to disloyalty are rarely aware of the nature of what they are participating in. As we shed light upon this area of darkness, may we gain the understanding and grace to renounce its deadly tentacles that seek to enslave our hearts.

# CHAPTER 19

# *What Is Disloyalty?*

N ow that we have looked carefully at what it means to be loyal to David, let's talk about disloyalty to David. Disloyalty is a horrible blight that undercuts families, churches, and businesses. Perhaps we can steer clear of it if we understand more clearly what it is.

There is a Bible word that helps to define disloyalty. It is rendered "treachery" or "disloyalty" depending on the translation. This word occurs in Judges 9:23, "God sent a spirit of ill will between Abimelech and the men of Shechem; and the men of Shechem dealt treacherously with Abimelech." While the New King James Version translates this Hebrew word as "treachery," or "treacherous," or "treacherously," the New International Version renders it as "disloyal," "traitor," "betrayed," and "betraying."[1]

This Hebrew word is used to describe how Jeremiah's natural brothers betrayed him: "'For even your brothers, the house of your father, even they have dealt treacherously with you; yes, they have called a multitude after you. Do not believe them, even though they speak smooth words to you'" (Jeremiah 12:6).

The Lord used the same word to express how the Israelites were disloyal to Him: "'But like men they transgressed the covenant; there they dealt treacherously with Me'" (Hosea 6:7).

My English dictionary defines the word treachery as, "Violation

---

[1] For examples, see the following verses in the NIV translation: Isaiah 24:16; 33:1; Jeremiah 12:6; Lamentations 1:2; Psalm 78:57.

of allegiance, confidence, or plighted faith; perfidy; treason."[2] The adjective, treacherous, is defined as, "Perfidious; likely to betray trust: unreliable."[3]

To be disloyal is to turn away from a relationship of mutual trust and do harm to the other. The harm can take the form of criticism, slander, backbiting, reproach, false witness, undermining, robbery, defamation, dishonor, personal attack, or something similar. *Disloyalty is not simply an absence of loyalty* (there are three categories: loyalty, an excellent spirit, and disloyalty). *Disloyalty steps beyond neutrality and somehow hurts the one with whom it was once aligned.*

### Disloyalty Is The Tip Of The Iceberg

Where disloyalty surfaces, don't be surprised if other vile things lie below the surface. That's because disloyalty is grown in the seedbed of our iniquitous hearts where a host of other evil propensities lurk. The surfacing of disloyalty is an indication that other iniquities have not been fully crucified. This truth is illustrated in the life of Ahithophel, one of David's longtime friends and primary confidants who, becoming swept up in Absalom's insurrection, conspired to kill David. Ahithophel was the primary person to whom David was referring when he wrote:

> For it is not an enemy who reproaches me; then I could bear it. Nor is it one who hates me who has exalted himself against me; then I could hide from him. But it was you, a man my equal, my companion and my acquaintance. We took sweet counsel together, and walked to the house of God in the throng. Let death seize them; let them go down alive into hell, for wickedness is in their dwellings and among them (Psalm 55:12-15).

This curse actually came upon Ahithophel, who committed suicide. David seems to suggest that where there is disloyalty, there are also other kinds of wickedness present in the heart ("for wickedness is in their dwellings and among them"). Ahithophel served righteously in David's court, but when he joined up with Absalom, all kinds of wickedness began to surface in his heart. For example, look at this

---

[2] Webster's New Collegiate Dictionary, G. & C. Merriam Company, Springield, MA, 1973, 1980.

[3] Ibid.

counsel he offered Absalom: "And Ahithophel said to Absalom, 'Go in to your father's concubines, whom he has left to keep the house; and all Israel will hear that you are abhorred by your father. Then the hands of all who are with you will be strong'" (2 Samuel 16:21). He actually counseled Absalom to have sex with his father's concubines! But even more than that, Ahithophel arranged for it to be done in broad daylight: "So they pitched a tent for Absalom on the top of the house, and Absalom went in to his father's concubines in the sight of all Israel" (2 Samuel 16:22). Absalom clearly had no heart to follow the law of his father's God, and Ahithophel was falling headlong with him into blatant ungodliness. When Ahithophel broke his loyalty to David, he also broke his loyalty to David's God.

While with David, this evil bent in Ahithophel's heart was never exposed. But once he aligned with Absalom, all kinds of wickedness began to pour from Ahithophel's heart. So disloyalty was not the only issue in Ahithophel; it was but the tip of the iceberg.

### Got A Problem With Your Leader?

*If you have a grievance with your leader, guard your tongue from spreading it to others.* Instead, go directly and privately to the leader in accordance with Matthew 18:15-17 and seek to gain your brother or sister. If you are unwilling to take this step, then hold your opinions to yourself in absolute silence.

*Disloyalty often finds a way to justify its non-compliance with Matthew 18:15-17.* It goes to others with its complaint, convinced that going to the father who has offended him is a useless effort. Matthew 18 is a safety mechanism against disloyalty, however, that could mollify disloyalty in its infancy stages if followed properly. But when Matthew 18 is not adhered to, disloyalty blossoms into a root of bitterness, becoming almost impossible to eradicate.

If you have a problem with David that cannot be resolved, don't stay in that ministry and raise trouble. Go to another territory and pursue what you feel God is giving you. "But my leader is a Saul!" someone might object. It makes no difference. Your duty is to relate to Saul as though he were David. Honor him as David, and do nothing to infringe upon or detract from his sphere of authority and influence.

Absalom had two options that could have saved him. He could

have stayed in Israel and accepted the sphere that David gave to him, enjoying the dignity of being the king's son; or he could have returned to the land of his mother, the land of Geshur, where his grandfather Talmai was king.[4] If he had pursued his ambitions in a foreign land he would have been much better off. But instead he chose to stay in his father's territory and tried to overthrow his father. It was the worst possible decision and it led to his downfall.

Sometimes, an untrue son will watch the Lord use him to bring correction or discipline to a spiritual father. He should watch in fear, however, because he may be next. Never forget that after God used the Chaldeans to discipline the Israelites, He judged the Chaldeans severely for their role in it. Just because God uses you to bring discipline to a spiritual father does not mean the Lord is pleased with you.

### How Disloyalty Operates

Disloyalty has certain telltale signs that are quite common wherever the spirit of Absalom is at work. Here are some of the ways disloyalty works.

1. **Disloyalty turns away from an established loyalty to David when David has not violated faith.**

   It's possible for a leader to do something that violates your trust in the relationship, and a withdrawal from loyalty in such instances may be understandable. But when we withdraw our loyalty because the relationship is no longer meeting our own personal goals and expectations, we're allowing our self-centeredness to pull us into disloyalty. You have loved David; will you leave him now for selfish reasons?

   We are warned about disloyalty that has no sound basis: "Woe to you who plunder, though you have not been plundered; and you who deal treacherously, though they have not dealt treacherously with you! When you cease plundering, you will be plundered; when you make an end of dealing treacherously, they will deal treacherously with you" (Isaiah 33:1). *Disloyalty and treachery carry their own inherent curse. You cannot violate loyalty without it coming back down on you.*

2. **Disloyalty spreads concerns, warnings, and negative opinions regarding the spiritual father.**

---

[4] 2 Samuel 3:3.

Another word for it is slander. Under the guise of caring for other believers, many have been guilty of slander without even realizing it. (Whenever we slander, we are oblivious to it; if we realized what we were doing, we would stop.) Slander poses as caring information, or helpful perspective, and it usually maligns David's motives. *Loyalty assumes the best in motives; slander presumes the worst in motives.*

Slander is incredibly devastating in the body of Christ. Its effects can undermine the work of God for many years to come. It's almost impossible to undo slander. How can you put toothpaste back into the tube? Once it's out, it's out. It's like blowing on a dandelion and then trying to regather the windblown seeds. It will never happen. The only cure for slander is to catch it before it's released.

Disloyalty is not simply disagreement. It is disagreement that insists on staying and undermining the leader's authority. Or it slanders the leader on its way out the door.

I heard recently of a sister who was very loyal to her pastor, and served as one of his personal intercessors, holding his hands up in vigilant prayer. A closeness and trust had been built over the years. But then someone who left the church spread his rancor to this sister, and it poisoned her against her pastor. She ended up leaving the church as well. Years of loyalty were torn down through slander, and the pastor lost a trusted armorbearer. "A perverse man sows strife, and a whisperer separates the best of friends" (Proverbs 16:28).

Slander can defile an entire local church. We are warned, "If anyone defiles the temple of God, God will destroy him. For the temple of God is holy, which temple you are" (1 Corinthians 3:17). What defiles the temple of God more rapidly than slander? Those who defile the work of God through slander run the risk of becoming disqualified and finding their destiny on earth destroyed by God.

Beware of secret whisperings. Jesus said, "'In secret I have said nothing'" (John 18:20). Slander usually says things it wouldn't want heard by the person being slandered. So here's a good question to ask to test for the presence of slander: "Would I be saying this, or listening to this, if the person about whom we're speaking were sharing in our conversation?" Don't say anything you wouldn't want shouted from the housetops. *A loyal person has no fear of being quoted because his words are always consistently loyal, whether spoken aloud or whispered.*

### 3. Disloyalty will attack David.

*Disloyalty comes against David personally.* Absalom is not content simply to spread slander about his father; he actually launches an assault against him.

The assault is usually in the form of accusation. It's one thing to confront in love because we want God's best for the other person; it's another thing to strike out in frustration. Disloyalty will lay stripes upon David. "And one will say to him, 'What are these wounds between your arms?' Then he will answer, 'Those with which I was wounded in the house of my friends'" (Zechariah 13:6).

In Absalom's case, he attempted to unseat David and assume his position.

Disloyalty does not involve merely rebutting false doctrine, or exposing the excesses within a certain movement or stream in the body of Christ. Disloyalty is almost always personal. It's a personal affront against an individual.

### 4. Disloyalty seeks to turn the hearts of the sons away from the father.

"This leader is dangerous!" they will say. "He's legalistic, controlling, and misleading."

Of course, it's possible for a leader to be all those things. That's why this subject of loyalty requires so much discernment and wisdom within the body of Christ. The Pharisees, thinking Jesus was dangerous and misleading, felt totally justified in their disloyalty to Him.

David would not stoop to try to turn anyone against Saul. Even though he could have felt justified in doing so, he never campaigned to turn people's hearts away from their king. He could have said, "I love the people too much to let them be carried away in Saul's errors." But by refusing to try to be a messiah to Saul's sons, David preserved an excellent spirit.

Those who campaign against a leader are very often wanting a following themselves. Paul warned us, "'Also from among yourselves men will rise up, speaking perverse things, to draw away the disciples after themselves'" (Acts 20:30). These men aren't saying, "I am your savior," nor are they saying, "Follow me." They're simply saying, "Follow Jesus—with us." Their desire to gather a following around themselves has the power to blind them to their disloyalty. If they had a true ministry calling, they would move far away and start over afresh. But these kinds of untrue sons don't tend to leave town quietly because, in their minds, they "care too much about the sheep." So they often stay nearby, undermine the father's authority, and receive those who choose to come under their wings.

Absalom has his own anointing—an anointing that is compelling enough to draw the undiscerning to himself. He is anointed with a leadership gifting, compassion, insight, boldness, and vision. His anointing is strong enough to lure someone as wise as Ahithophel into the conspiracy. *Look at those in his ranks and you'll find mostly those who were spiritual sons of David.*

## 5. Disloyalty will not cover the father.

All of us make mistakes and have those moments when we need our associates to cover us in love and not broadcast our weaknesses abroad. "'Love will cover a multitude of sins'" (1 Peter 4:8). Because it has lost its love, disloyalty will expose rather than cover the father's weaknesses.

Here's an illustration of this truth from Noah's life.

And Noah began to be a farmer, and he planted a vineyard. Then he drank of the wine and was drunk, and became uncovered in his tent. And Ham, the father of Canaan, saw the nakedness of his father, and told his two brothers outside. But Shem and Japheth took a garment, laid it on both their shoulders, and went backward and covered the nakedness of their father. Their faces were turned away, and they did not see their father's nakedness. So Noah awoke from his wine, and knew what his younger son had done to him. Then he said: "Cursed be Canaan; a servant of servants he shall be to his brethren." And he said: "Blessed be the LORD, the God of Shem, and may Canaan be his servant" (Genesis 9:20-26).

Ham was the untrue son in this story. When he saw his father's nakedness exposed, he went and told others. "Guys, take a look at this!" Shem and Japheth were the true sons in the story—they covered their father in his moment of weakness and exposure. Noah's curse on

Canaan, Ham's son, seems pretty strong, but it's Noah's response to Ham's disloyalty. Through betrayal, Ham's posterity forfeited much of their inheritance.

*Loyal sons protect the reputation of their father; disloyal sons spill little secrets about the father that undermine his credibility or make him the brunt of laughter.*

### Speaking The Truth

One of the favorite verses of the one assaulting David is Ephesians 4:15, "But, speaking the truth in love, may grow up in all things into Him who is the head—Christ." Disloyalty often flies under the banner of "truth." *The disloyal son sees himself as the standard-bearer of truth.*

Truth, in the hand of a disloyal son, becomes a sword that gashes and wounds. Instead of serving the father, it dismembers him.

Loyalty, in contrast, operates under a strong, healthy fear of the Lord, remembering that He said, "'Do not touch My anointed ones, and do My prophets no harm'" (Psalm 105:15).

Joab was faced with a difficult choice on one occasion: Go with truth, or go with David. He knew that David was wrong in wanting to number the people (David was violating clear guidelines in Moses' law), and yet David was his leader. In the end, Joab chose to honor David's place of authority and release David to be straightened out by God. In that particular instance, it was a wise move. In some cases, it's important to stand for truth. But in Joab's case, had he stood for truth, he would have crossed over into disloyalty.

Joab had to choose between truth and submission. Which was the higher value in the situation at hand? That is a pivotally important question. Disloyalty is often the result of a wrong judgment call when having to choose between conflicting values.

### *For Group Discussion*

1.  Where there is disloyalty, what other evils do you think could be operating in someone's heart?

2.  Look at Matthew 18:15-17. How could adherence to this passage help to militate against disloyalty?

3.  Have you noticed how a strong anointing can sometimes rest upon the one who is breeding disloyalty? Why does God sometimes anoint the Absaloms?

4.  Launching from Joab's example, talk about the tension between truth and submission. In a time of conflicting values, which virtue takes precedence?

# CHAPTER 20

## *Seeds Of Disloyalty*

**W**hat causes disloyalty to germinate and spring up? It is always the result of sinful desires that have not been surrendered completely to the cross and dealt the death blow. For example, the desire to gather a following around oneself—as mentioned earlier—is a sinful desire that will produce betrayal and treachery if not crucified. Let's consider some of the causative factors for disloyalty.

**1. Disloyalty is often the result of unresolved disappointment or bitterness in one's past.**

This is the foremost cause of disloyalty, and it's seen clearly in Absalom's life. Absalom had a grudge toward his father that went back many years, and when he did not deal properly with his grievance by forgiving his father, that bitter root grew into a tree of treachery.

Offences are unavoidable. Jesus warned us, "'And then many will be offended, will betray one another, and will hate one another'" (Matthew 24:10). Virtually all of us have been wounded, rejected, hurt, or violated. If these things are unresolved, then the seeds of disloyalty lie dormant within us, waiting for the right circumstances to germinate.

Some saints carry an underlying suspicion toward authority, sometimes rooted in their relationship to their parents or other authority figures in their past. Because of unresolved issues in their heart, they always have difficulty submitting themselves fully to leaders in authority. All it takes is for the right circumstances to surface and they will launch on what they're convinced is a righteous campaign against David.

Absalom will always claim that David has violated him. He will persuade others because he is both convincing and sincere. This causes David much soul searching. But in the final analysis, the problem is not David's poor people skills but Absalom's bitter spirit. David handles Absalom imperfectly but keeps chasing God; Absalom, on the other hand, grows bitter because he has never died to his own ambitions.

We don't know when Absalom's bitterness first took root. We do know, however, that his first act of disloyalty was not in trying to take his father's throne. It happened many years earlier when he took justice into his own hands and murdered his half-brother, Amnon. Murdering Amnon was a direct act of disloyalty against his father, David. When Absalom killed his brother, he put a knife through his father's heart. It was an indicator of Absalom's disregard for his father even back then. David loved Absalom so very dearly,[1] and yet for some reason the love was not reciprocated.

My father, Arvin Sorge, says that *an offended person is a potential traitor*, a principle that is seen clearly in Judas Iscariot's life. When Jesus rebuked Judas's carnal responses, he became offended. His offence eventually manifested in betrayal.

Disloyalty would be far less common in the body of Christ if we were to pray daily, "'For we also forgive everyone who is indebted to us'" (Luke 11:4).

## 2. Disloyalty can stem from an inability to receive correction.

David tried to administer discipline to Absalom for murdering his brother Amnon. It's questionable whether David disciplined Absalom perfectly, but his intentions were right. However, Absalom never received it.

*Disloyal sons feel that the father's discipline is harsh and unreasonable.* David's heart intentions are seen through a cynical lens.

Absalom chafes under his father's restraints. Like a kite in the wind, Absalom strains against the way his father holds him back. When Absalom finally breaks free of his father, he suddenly recognizes that it was his father's rootedness that gave him the ability to soar. Now, like a kite with no moorings, his aspirations all come crashing to the ground.

---

[1] See 2 Samuel 18:33; 19:4.

### 3. Disloyalty is sometimes caused by unrealistic expectations the son places upon the father.

It would appear that Judas was not pleased with the way Jesus was discipling him. *When a father does not satisfy a son's desires to be fathered properly, it's possible for the son's disappointment to culminate in disloyalty.*

Mentoring relationships seem to suffer damage frequently by unfulfilled expectations. The son enters into relationship with the spiritual father with hopes of life-transforming impartation. When the son doesn't receive what he had envisioned, it's tempting to assign blame to the father.

What sons must understand is that the nature of a father/son relationship in the Kingdom will always be determined by the father, not the son. The father's giftings and personality will set the pace for how the relationship goes. A true son will appreciate and enjoy the father for who he is and allow the relationship to find its own organic entity.

Young men today might think, "Boy, I sure wish I had been Timothy, and had Paul as my spiritual father!" If you were Timothy, you probably would be disappointed at the level of input coming from Paul. Paul didn't have time for fireside chats. If you wanted to absorb anything from Paul's life, you had to do it while being tossed on the open seas and shipwrecked with him. "Run with me, Timothy, keep your eyes and ears open, and catch what you can."

*My point is, sons can easily glamorize what a true father/son relationship should be. When the relationship doesn't meet their high standards, disloyalty is knocking on their door.* In their immaturity, sons come to the relationship primarily for their own personal benefit. If it doesn't satisfy their felt needs, it's tempting to be off in pursuit of another place to land.

One reason I'm writing like this is with the hope that some readers will awaken to the seeds of disloyalty that have been at work in their heart and make a turnaround. Disloyal sons do not, like Cain, have an indelible mark on them. We can awaken to our mistakes and repent. We need not despair over our failures. There is grace from God to repent and pursue a loyal spirit again. Thank God, He gives us new beginnings!

### Abimelech's Disloyalty

Abimelech was a young man in the Bible who was disloyal to his father, Gideon, because of unresolved bitterness in his past. It's a fascinating story with some instructive implications, so please let me tell it.

Abimelech's father, Gideon, was one of the great warriors of the Bible, even mentioned in the Hebrews 11 "hall of faith." Gideon had galvanized the nation of Israel against the Midianites who had been oppressing Israel, and led them to a dynamic victory. He continued to judge the nation of Israel faithfully for 40 years after that mighty deliverance. During that time, he fathered many sons, including a son that was born to one of his female servants[2] who became Gideon's concubine.[3] She must have felt ostracized by Gideon's other wives for some reason because she chose to live in a totally different city (Shechem). As a result, Abimelech grew up under reproach, feeling like an outcast all his life. He had no relationship with his father, Gideon. Abimelech was neither numbered with Gideon's 70 sons, nor did he live with them. So rejection and bitterness lie at the root of his story.

After Gideon died, the men of Shechem (in Abimelech's home town) made Abimelech their ruler. Abimelech gathered a group of ruffians, rose up, and killed all of his 70 brothers. Only the youngest escaped. After Gideon had served Israel for so many years, Abimelech committed the ultimate act of treachery against his father by killing his half-brothers.

Being dead, Gideon obviously could do nothing about Abimelech's disloyalty. But God took it all in, and God Himself set his face against Abimelech.

> After Abimelech had reigned over Israel three years, God sent a spirit of ill will between Abimelech and the men of Shechem; and the men of Shechem dealt treacherously with Abimelech, that the crime done to the seventy sons of Jerubbaal might be settled and their blood be laid on Abimelech their brother, who killed them, and on the men of Shechem, who aided him in the killing of his brothers (Judges 9:22-24).

Abimelech and the men of Shechem had come into an alliance

[2] Judges 9:18.
[3] Judges 8:31.

that was founded upon disloyalty to Gideon. So God targeted the ill-founded alliance, caused it to collapse after three years, and turned the loyalties of the men of Shechem away from Abimelech to a man named Gaal.

In response, Abimelech and his men attacked the city of Shechem and killed the entire population.

At a later battle, Abimelech was wounded by a millstone dropped on his head, and he died.

The Scripture's commentary on those events is that "God repaid the wickedness of Abimelech, which he had done to his father by killing his seventy brothers, and all the evil of the men of Shechem God returned on their own heads" (Judges 9:56-57). So all those involved in the unholy alliance founded in disloyalty were repaid by God and suffered untimely deaths.

Abimelech's story is a textbook case of bitterness turned into disloyalty. But his bitterness toward his father, Gideon, was not confined to himself. He spread it to the inhabitants of Shechem and all of Israel. Influenced by Abimelech, the people of Israel dishonored Gideon's fatherly role among them. Consequently, the nation suffered bitterly.

Abimelech's example constrains us to ask ourselves this poignant question: Have we adequately honored those who, both in the past and present, have fathered and mothered in our midst? Some leaders are but one in a string of many who have served over the years; but there are some leaders who have *fathered* in a locale. God reserves a blessing for us when we honor our Gideons. "'Honor your father and mother,' which is the first commandment with promise: 'that it may be well with you and you may live long on the earth'" (Ephesians 6:2-3).

### For Group Discussion

1. Does your group agree that disloyalty is most commonly rooted in unresolved bitterness? Share an incident in which you had to release a bitterness that could have corrupted your heart. Or talk about a bitterness that you're still striving to overcome.

2. Talk about the kite illustration. Have you known a son who has pulled against the constraints placed upon him?

3. How can we guard against forming unrealistic expectations in a mentoring relationship?

4. What stands out most to you in the Abimelech story?

# CHAPTER 21

## *How To Avoid Betrayal*

**B**y now, we're all ready to avoid disloyalty and betrayal at almost any cost. So what steps can we take to guard against or ensure that we will not become the victims of disloyalty and betrayal from those around our lives?

The answer is quite simple, really. The surest safeguard against betrayal is this: *Don't have any sons.* Do not seek to reproduce yourself or to invest in the next generation. Fly solo. Trust no one. Have no sons—either natural or spiritual sons—and you will have the least chance of being betrayed.

Once you decide you want a posterity, however, the chances of your sons' being disloyal to you rise exponentially.

If David had had no sons, he would not have experienced the rebellion of Absalom and Adonijah. But then again, nor would he have known the joy of setting his progeny, Solomon, on the throne.

If Jesus had had no disciples, He would not have tasted the kiss of betrayal. Nor would he have passed the baton to a group of disciples who, following in His steps, turned their world upsidedown.

*Disloyalty and betrayal are the inherent risks a spiritual father takes when he invests in spiritual sons.* Love places us in the palm of another's hand, where we are moved by the other's love and stung by the other's rejection. The opening of the heart that embraces a son and brings him into the inner circle of confidence is the very opening that gives the disloyal son the opportunity for betrayal. If the son wasn't loved so, it wouldn't hurt so.

I was a guest speaker once in a church where, after the meeting, the pastor told me of a warning he had received from someone in his church regarding one of his leaders. A brother with a prophetic gifting warned this pastor that a certain leader in the church was eventually going to stir dissension and cause a church split, taking a group away with him. To date that had not happened, and the pastor was asking for my counsel. It was admittedly difficult for him not to be suspicious of this leader from that point on.

I pointed to the Scripture that says love "believes all things" (1 Corinthians 13:7), so love believes the best in others. Love does not live in suspicion of those on one's leadership team. A word of warning like this is not a basis for withholding ministry from a qualified vessel. But on the other hand, wisdom does not despise a prophecy given in the name of Jesus.[1]

If the prophecy is true, then I wondered together with the pastor what God's purpose might be in giving the warning. Would it be so that the pastor could protect himself against potential disloyalty? I don't think so—neither David nor Jesus protected themselves. If the word is true, I don't think it was given for the pastor's sake, but for the sake of the young leader. Perhaps the Spirit gave it so that this pastor could provide informed leadership to this young man, giving him every opportunity to turn from the treachery of his heart. This is how Jesus handled Judas. Knowing what was in Judas's heart, Jesus still invited Judas onto His leadership team, and over a three-year period gave him every possible opportunity to deal with the issues of his heart. At the Passover meal, knowing Judas would betray Him that night, Jesus washed his feet. And then, in an act of ultimate mercy, Jesus even stepped forward at His arrest to identify Himself, removing from before Judas the necessity to offer the kiss of betrayal.[2] What a Leader!

[1] 1 Thessalonians 5:20.
[2] See John 18:5.

*For Group Discussion*

1. When you consider the risks, why is spiritual fatherhood still worth it?

2. If you were being warned that someone on your team was going to be disloyal to you, like the pastor was warned in this chapter's story, how would you respond? Consider what happened to Gedaliah when he didn't believe the report of the treachery that was formulated against him (Jeremiah 40:7-41:3).

# CHAPTER 22

# *How Should We Respond to Disloyalty?*

W hen a leader sees disloyalty brewing, should he confront it directly or allow the Lord to defend Him? There is a time for everything. There is a time to leave Judas alone and allow him to reveal his true colors. There is also a time for immediate, decisive action.

Jesus indicated He has quite a severe manner of dealing with those who are disloyal to Him: "'But bring here those enemies of mine, who did not want me to reign over them, and slay them before me'" (Luke 19:27). Jesus deals this vehemently with disloyalty because it has absolutely no place in the eternal city. Disloyalty, unless handled with this kind of finality, always brews trouble. Undealt with, it is like leaven that works through the dough.

When we are aware of the leaven of disloyalty at work in the body of Christ, we are counseled to deal with it radically: "Therefore purge out the old leaven, that you may be a new lump, since you truly are unleavened" (1 Corinthian 5:7). The words "purge out" describe the kind of thoroughness a surgeon uses in getting all the cancer out of a patient's body. A similar caution is provided in Hebrews 12:15, "Looking carefully lest anyone fall short of the grace of God; lest any root of bitterness springing up cause trouble, and by this many become defiled." We are to look carefully so that we might defuse disloyalty before it explodes.

It is dangerous, however, to confront disloyalty prematurely, for it can produce heightened tension in the camp instead of resolve. Jesus addressed this in Matthew 13:24-30, when He said that it's possible to extract the false while doing damage to the genuine. One cannot successfully remove tares from the midst until it becomes evident to all observers that the tares are, in fact, just that. If the tares are confronted prematurely, the undiscerning will think you are pulling up wheat. In other words, if you try to remove it before it is clear to the main players that disloyalty is truly the problem, you hazard causing more damage relationally among the genuine members than if you left it alone and waited for the thing to come to a ripe head.

And what should a believer do who sees disloyalty in another believer? Paul's counsel was, "From such people turn away!" (see 2 Timothy 3:2, 5).

There is a time when disloyalty should be allowed no quarter but should be expunged decisively. David himself did not deal with those who were disloyal to him; but he did instruct his son, Solomon, to use wisdom in dispensing justice to them. Solomon did just that. When the right occasion surfaced, Solomon sent Benaiah to execute Adonijah, who had attempted David's overthrow. Then Joab was executed for participating in Adonijah's treason. Then Abiathar, the priest, was removed from the priesthood for his collusion and sent home to his farm. And finally, Shimei, the Benjamite who railed upon David as he fled from Absalom, violated the terms of his confinement in Jerusalem and was duly executed. When those four men, who had come to represent disloyalty to David, were removed by Solomon, the Scripture then testified, "Thus the kingdom was established in the hand of Solomon" (1 Kings 2:46). Solomon was not totally established on his throne until he had dealt with the elements of disloyalty in his kingdom.

There *is* a time to deal with disloyalty in the ranks.

### Can A Leader Mend Torn Loyalties?

If the sons' loyalties toward their spiritual father have suffered loss, can the father do anything to repair the damage? Let's answer that question by looking at Paul's relationship to the church at Corinth.

The Corinthian believers were initially loyal to Paul, but then a certain faction rose up in the spirit of Absalom that tried to undermine that relationship. Paul did not sit by quietly, however, and allow it to progress unchallenged. He knew it was in the best interests of the Corinthians to remain true to him because he would serve them as a faithful father. So for their sakes he chose to confront the thing. He sought to repair their allegiance before it became outright disloyalty.

Here's how Paul fought for it: *He appealed to them in love.* He didn't invoke his apostolic authority and demand their loyalty. Rather, he pled for their love. "Open your hearts to us. We have wronged no one, we have corrupted no one, we have cheated no one" (2 Corinthians 7:2).

He wasn't saying, "Be loyal to us because we're better leaders than others." In fact, Paul was careful to emphasize that there was nothing inherent to themselves that was sufficient for anything; their sufficiency was from God.[1] Rather, he was appealing for their love because God had placed him in their lives in that ministry of oversight,[2] he loved them dearly,[3] and he was jealous to present them as a chaste virgin to Christ.[4]

*To express love and appeal for love is the closest one can get to asking for loyalty.*

In the case of the Corinthians, Paul's approach was successful. He spoke later of how they affirmed their loyalty to him: "For observe this very thing, that you sorrowed in a godly manner: What diligence it produced in you, what clearing of yourselves, what indignation, what fear, what vehement desire, what zeal, what vindication! In all things you proved yourselves to be clear in this matter" (2 Corinthians 7:11). They had shown vehement desire to express their fidelity to Paul; and in fear they dealt with the divisive brother who had sought to turn their loyalties away from Paul. It was in this manner that the Corinthians vindicated themselves.

Paul went on to say, "Therefore, although I wrote to you, I did not do it for the sake of him who had done the wrong, nor for the sake of him who suffered wrong, but that our care for you in the sight of God might appear to you" (2 Corinthians 7:12). Above all, Paul wanted them to realize how much he loved them.

Paul's response of love included his love for the brother who was disloyal. Similarly, Jesus loved Judas unceasingly. David likewise loved Absalom to the end. Even when we must confront disloyalty, may the

[1] 2 Corinthians 3:5-6.
[2] 2 Corinthians 10:13.
[3] 2 Corinthians 7:12.
[4] 2 Corinthians 11:2.

Lord give us fervent love for those who are erring.

### How Should I Relate To Friends Who Have Been Disloyal?

Let's suppose your friend has been disloyal to you. You have done your utmost to repair the rift, but it was beyond your control, and now disloyalty has produced a clear breach in your relationship. Now what do you do?

The sad truth is, where disloyalty has severed a friendship, in most cases the breach is never repaired. The only way for that to be different would be for God Himself to step into the situation and turn the heart of the disloyal party back to the one who was violated.

Occasionally, God will do this. For example, in Job's case, God intervened by speaking directly to Eliphaz (one of Job's three friends) and instructing him to return to Job for a prayer of blessing.

And so it was, after the LORD had spoken these words to Job, that the LORD said to Eliphaz the Temanite, "My wrath is aroused against you and your two friends, for you have not spoken of Me what is right, as My servant Job has. Now therefore, take for yourselves seven bulls and seven rams, go to My servant Job, and offer up for yourselves a burnt offering; and My servant Job shall pray for you. For I will accept him, lest I deal with you according to your folly; because you have not spoken of Me what is right, as My servant Job has." So Eliphaz the Temanite and Bildad the Shuhite and Zophar the Naamathite went and did as the LORD commanded them; for the LORD had accepted Job (Job 42:7-9).

If God had not sovereignly stepped into that breach, it would have never been repaired on its own. It was God's mercy to turn them back to Job because they had actually come under the wrath of God for their disloyalty. God could have allowed the three friends to become hardened in their position and reap the consequences. But instead, God had mercy upon their ignorance by revealing to Eliphaz His displeasure.

But God doesn't step sovereignly like this into every breach. What happened between Lot and Abraham is much more common: Lot never returned to Abraham.

In another example, the leaders of Israel were disloyal to the prophet Jeremiah, even though Jeremiah had faithfully delivered to them the word of the Lord. Their response to Jeremiah's faithfulness was to abuse and imprison him. And here's how the Lord counseled Jeremiah to handle it: "'Let them return to you, but you must not return to them'" (Jeremiah 15:19). God was basically saying, "If this breach is ever to be healed, it is the responsibility of those who have been disloyal to you to approach you first. Don't you approach them. If you do, your efforts will be fruitless and counter-productive. Wait for their hearts to return to you. If they return to you, embrace them; if they don't return to you, love them and release them to Me."

### Perceiving Redemptive Purpose In Disloyalty

Disloyalty is intensely painful to spiritual fathers and mothers. It has the power to take the wind entirely out of their sails. They can become so distracted in trying to manage the relational chaos that the cause of Christ suffers for it. And of course, this is part of the enemy's agenda in stirring up betrayal, for he knows how devastating it is to the Kingdom of God.

In the wake of Absalom's treason, everyone seemingly suffered loss. Absalom lost; David lost; Joab lost; David's concubines lost; Amasa lost; Ahithophel lost; Shimei lost; Mephibosheth lost; Sheba lost; and the entire nation suffered. No one emerged a winner (which is why disloyalty must be resisted so tenaciously in the church today). And yet, God has a way of turning even betrayal into a tool of refinement for His Davids. God can bring honey out of the rock.

David saw disloyalty as part of God's training in his life. It was necessary for him to taste of its gall so that he could be a sign, personally, of the betrayal that the coming Messiah would experience. Furthermore, David's betrayal qualified him to speak to every subsequent generation of leaders. To be a prototype leader—a forerunner—David had to experience the full orb of rejection that leaders face. His example as a leader would be far less relevant if he had never had an untrue son.

Now we're able to see it so clearly: *Wherever there's a David, there's an Absalom. Absalom just comes as part of the package.* Absalom is one of the ways God keeps David meek and humble in the midst of promotion and great spiritual victories. God has a purpose in the betrayal, and it's mightily important that David see God's hand in it so that he can relate to the wayward son in brokenness, meekness, and mercy.

God uses everything. Even the most negative things are redeemed for His purposes. He takes advantage of every fragment "'so that nothing is lost'" (John 6:12). *God doesn't instigate disloyalty against David, but when it surfaces He uses it to train and fashion him, and to keep him soft and dependent and humble.*

### For Group Discussion

1.  What do you think—should we excise disloyalty immediately or wait for God to defend us?
2.  Can you think of a time when you saw an appeal for love that truly worked?
3.  Has anyone ever been disloyal to you? How did you respond?
4.  What do you believe are some of the redemptive purposes God can bring out of disloyalty?

# PART FOUR
## *Hearts Of Fathers Turned To The Children*

Finally, let's examine an area that is so dear to the heart of God: The partnering of the generations for the sake of the great endtime harvest. Loyalty is at the center of the Spirit's call for the generations to be joined together in affection and shared purpose—because Christ's return is nearer than ever, even at the door.

# CHAPTER 23

## *Honoring The Father's Sphere*

L oyalty is largely (although not exclusively) an issue between generations. It's the noble bond that joins one generation to another.

We are living in a unique time in history—a time when God is turning the hearts of fathers to their children and children to their fathers. God is placing within today's generation a passionate desire to be loyal to their spiritual fathers.

If you're under age 30 and have just finished the previous section on disloyalty, you probably are experiencing a profound desire in your heart to be loyal to the fathers and mothers of the older generation. This is awesome! God is preparing your heart.

In this concluding section, therefore, I will try to paint a picture of where God is leading our hearts in loyalty, how we will get there, and what it will look like.

### *Loyalty Honors Sphere*

In Chapter 2, we dealt with Paul's usage of the word "sphere."[1] Sphere is the circle of influence among people that God gives to a man or woman. Because it's given of God, no one can add significantly to it, and no one should try to take away from it. Loyalty will never undermine the sphere of a spiritual father or mother. This truth is step one in walking forward together.

Paul made an interesting request of the Corinthian believers. He

---

[1] 2 Corinthians 10:13-16.

expressed his hope that they would enlarge him in his sphere.[2] He wasn't asking them to enlarge his sphere—no man could do that. But he was asking them to give him, open-handedly, the privilege and right of functioning in their midst with full apostolic authority.

He was appealing to their loyalty by basically saying, "God has placed you in our sphere; you are in our hearts to live together and to die together. Please recognize the role God has given us in your lives, receive us with open hearts, and allow us to function fully within our God-given sphere." The issue in loyalty is opening your heart wide to that person. There was an Absalom spirit at work in Corinth to steal from Paul his place of apostolic authority and oversight in the church. To counter that spirit, He could not demand or ask for their loyalty, but he could appeal for their love.

To enlarge Paul greatly in his own sphere, the Corinthians would need to say to him things like, "Paul, we recognize that your sphere includes us because you came to us with the gospel. We owe our lives to the sacrifice of your labors among us. Therefore, we welcome your fatherly input into our lives. We actively seek your spiritual covering and oversight, and purpose to do our best to follow all that you ask of us. We give our hearts in this way because we have seen your love for us, and now we reciprocate by assuring you of our loving affections for you. We love and trust you because we know your life is totally poured out for the sake of the Kingdom and our mutual edification. Our hearts are yours. We will give you even greater honor in our midst than we have in the past because we're convinced that as we honor your role over us and among us that we will be blessed of God. We will honor and enlarge your place of authority with us, and then will release you to go to the unreached peoples of Spain."

Paul's sphere did not extend to every city and church that existed in his time, but only to those churches where he had a personal history of building. Those churches that recognized and honored Paul's sphere among them did so to their own edification and safety.

Paul did not see his sphere as a realm in which he enjoyed superior privileges because of his seniority. He did not use his apostolic sphere as an opportunity to exert power over people or fleece their financial reserves. Rather, he modeled Christlike leadership by washing the feet

[2] 2 Corinthians 10:15.

of those in his sphere. He labored more abundantly that they might enter into abundant life. Rather than ruling over them as a king who enjoyed a higher station in life, Paul poured out his life for them as the servant of all.

The apostles will be honored in their sphere as they lay their lives down for the gospel. Paul said the apostles were appointed first[3] but exhibited last.[4] In other words, apostles are first in authority and last in privilege. Apostles don't use their authority to get the sons to do their work for them. For their sphere and authority to be embraced, apostles have to work more, give more, bear more, and pray more. The sons aren't given to the apostle to make the apostle look good; it's the other way around. The greater David's sphere, the less he takes and the more he gives. As someone once said, if you want your men to bleed, you have to hemorrhage.

It bears repeating: Loyalty is always very aware of sphere. A true son will always be cognizant of the father's domain and will do nothing to violate that sphere. Because he was loyal to Paul, Timothy never did anything to infringe upon Paul's sphere. Rather, he was always careful to remain within his own sphere and preserve for Paul that which was properly his. Paul noticed how Timothy did this*, and that's why he called him a true son.

*A true son does not usurp anything of his father's in order to establish his own sphere.* An untrue son, in contrast, feels that the father's sphere is overshadowing and constrictive. An untrue son sees himself as a small sapling in the shade of a huge oak, and as long as the father (the oak) is in place, the young sapling will never have opportunity to catch the light of the sun and grow into his own destiny. He concludes, therefore, that if he is going to grow, the father must be cut down or somehow be removed. The untrue son thus ends up violating his loyalty to his father in favor of trying to establish his own sphere.

### Honoring David's Sphere Produces Blessings

A true father should not be viewed as a large tree that shuts down the growth of everything beneath him; rather, *he is like a nutritious vine, and all who join themselves to him will benefit from the flow of life*

[3] 1 Corinthians 12:28.
[4] 1 Corinthians 4:9.

*that is generated through his ministry.* The greater the father's sphere, the more branches (sons and daughters) that can be joined to him. Great spiritual fathers provide a spiritual covering under which many sons and daughters can flourish and develop into their destiny.

David's kingdom is a marvelous illustration of this truth. Those who expressed allegiance to David were made captains of troops.[5] Had they been disloyal to David, they would have never risen to such places of great authority and stewardship in the kingdom. Because they were loyal, they found themselves serving prominently in a nation that grew to become the greatest monarchy on the globe at the time.

Timothy experienced the same thing. By honoring Paul's sphere, Timothy came into a breadth of ministry that was far greater than anything he would have ever touched on his own.

### Disloyalty Challenges David's Sphere

When God starts to bless a company because of their loyalty to David, and great wars are won by Joab and his captains, it's very tempting for those captains to begin to think that the growth and extension of the nation is due to their battle prowess and expertise. It's easy for them to believe that they are responsible for the great victories. Then, when David exercises a degree of authority they don't like, they can become disgruntled and begin to think, "Hey, David, you're not indispensable. If you're not careful, we'll get rid of you because we don't need you to maintain the momentum we're enjoying."

In cases where the captains do get rid of David, however, they soon discover that the blessings they've been enjoying have been because they've been under the egis of David's authority. God is in covenant with David and is helping him, and they've been enjoying the fruitfulness of being connected to David's vine. If they remove themselves from David's sphere, God is no longer helping them as He once did, and things eventually take a negative turn.

When Absalom pushed into David's sphere, David relinquished it and fled from Jerusalem. David's perspective was, "God gave me my sphere, and if I am ever to have it again, God will give it back to me." *Knowing that his sphere was God-given, David was not possessive but re-*

---

[5] 1 Chronicles 12:18.

*leasing.* He waited for God's vindication, which God did by restoring him to the throne.

You don't ever have to limit someone else's sphere in order to establish your own sphere of influence. The Kingdom works exactly the opposite. *You will find your greatest inheritance when you contend for the spheres of your companions to be enlarged to their fullest measure.*

### Helping Timothy Find His Sphere

The wisest thing a son can do is stay in rank beneath his father, remain true in love, and accept the spheres of authority that come to him under the father's covering. In this manner, he will uncover a much greater inheritance and will be saved some very painful bumps and bruises along the way.

Some people think that if Paul is to help Timothy find his place in the harvest, that Paul should step aside and stop harvesting so that Timothy can come into his own. This is not true fatherhood. *Paul fathers Timothy by harvesting at a maximum pace while training Timothy at his side.* The loyal son *wants* the father to function, knowing that this model is most efficient both in terms of gathering the harvest and training the true sons.

Timothy, here's my advice to you: Find a spiritual father who will set a pace for you, then get behind him and swing your sickle on the momentum of the swath he's cutting. *Honor his sphere, and he'll take you places you've never seen before.*

### Releasing The Endtime Apostles

*When God's Davids are honored and enlarged in their sphere, the entire body of Christ benefits because those with an apostolic mandate are released to function.* God is doing a marvelous thing in the earth today. He is raising up Davids and Pauls (male and female) with apostolic callings on their lives, who are being commissioned of God to lead the body of Christ forward in her endtime mandates. While David himself may not feel much liberty to speak of loyalty to his team (lest he appear self-serving), the fact is that it plays possibly the most critical role in releasing him into the fullness of his calling.

Loyalty has no greater joy than when David is honored, esteemed, extolled, awarded, promoted, enlarged, and given a greater sphere.

When factions of disloyalty come against David, they hurt both themselves and the progress of the Kingdom. We look back at those who rose up against David and we just want to say to them, "What are you thinking? Do you understand the privilege you have, of serving under David? Why aren't you maximizing this opportunity?"

They would probably retort, "David's reputation has taken on mythological proportions. You don't understand, he is incredibly human. Living with him is not as nice as the storybooks paint it. The guy is a royal pain at times. Either we play the game his way, or we don't play at all. It's repressive!"

"No, *you* don't get it!" we would reply. "You don't realize how good you've got it. All you'd have to do is step into another era and look back, and you'd realize what an unusual privilege you have to serve with such a great leader."

Most Davids aren't fully recognized and appreciated until they're dead. It is the fate of the Absaloms to ever look back on what could have been and regret their myopic choices.

### The Power Of Release

*Loyalty releases authority.* Timothy's loyalty gave Paul authority in his life. Loyalty is a powerful thing, for it establishes nobility in the son's heart and calls forth nobility in the father's heart. Loyalty directed to an immature leader can actually empower that leader to grow into his or her potential. And it also has the power to transform the follower in the process. It turned depressed, disgruntled debtors into David's mighty men. The greatest leaders are surrounded by people who are as human as anybody else—but loyalty has lifted them up to the nobility of greatness.

Loyalty will be one of the critical factors in determining when the endtime apostles are released in the body of Christ. If leaders will be loyal to their apostles, the apostles will be empowered to function. It is critical that the endtime Bride find this loyalty to her Davids, because the scheme of the enemy will be to sow discord among brothers. Without loyalty, the apostles will be hindered and thwarted; with the apostles bound, the surging momentum of the church will be thwarted. It is the release of the apostles that will catapult the church forward into her endtime inheritance.

**For Group Discussion**

1.  What does enlarging your spiritual father's sphere mean to you?
2.  When you look at spiritual fathers, have you seen large oaks that constrict the growth of everything beneath them, or have you seen fruitful vines that promote the growth of everything attached to them?
3.  Have you a Timothy whom you are trying to guide into his own sphere of ministry effectiveness? Who? How are you approaching that?
4.  To see the release of God's endtime apostles sounds wonderful to all of us! But what can we do to facilitate their release?

# CHAPTER 24

## *Endowing True Sons*

G od created the entire universe for one simple purpose: to bring many sons to glory. God has the heart of a true Father—He has created all things for His sons. My parents have an expression they use frequently, "Everything for the kids!" This is the heart of our Father God as well. We are literally the center of His universe.

### *Endowing Fathers, Enriched Sons*

Fathers do everything for the sons. As noted in Chapter 15, the role of the fathers is to enrich the sons. For example, the Father's plan in redemption was to enrich His Son:

> Therefore God also has highly exalted Him and given Him the name which is above every name, that at the name of Jesus every knee should bow, of those in heaven, and of those on earth, and of those under the earth, and that every tongue should confess that Jesus Christ is Lord, to the glory of God the Father (Philippians 2:9-11).

The Father has enriched the Son by giving Him not only all the wealth of heaven, but also giving Him a name above every other name.

The role of the sons is to glory in and glorify the father. That's why Jesus said to His Father, "'I have glorified You on the earth'" (John 17: 4). *The Son gets the endowment, and the Father gets the glory. So everyone comes away wowed at the Father.*

This same pattern holds true for fathers and sons in the faith. The sons come away enriched; but what makes it safe for them is that the fathers come away with the glory in the relationship. The sons are made rich, and the fathers get all the credit.

In Absalom's case, he wasn't satisfied with just the riches; he also wanted the glory. That's the nature of disloyalty—it doesn't simply want the father's endowment; it also wants the father's sphere. When the father receives the glory, that's what saves the son from being destroyed by his enrichment. Absalom cannot see that he is safest when David gets the glory.

The son who is loyal—Solomon—will eventually come into his own glory when David passes on. It's not until the passing of a generation that Solomon will be established in the glory of fatherhood, with his own sons under him. Because he is patient, Solomon will see that day; being impetuous, Absalom will never see it.

*True fathers long to endow their sons so they can be launched toward their promises.* This would explain David's anguish over Absalom. David longed to give Absalom the utmost that he could in order to move Absalom toward his destiny. But David also knew, in his wisdom, that if he gave Absalom too much too soon, it could eventuate in his ruin.

David withheld strategically from both Solomon and Absalom, waiting for the right time. Solomon saw his father withholding the throne from him, but his response was one of loyalty. He waited patiently. Absalom, on the other hand, saw his father withholding from him, and he responded in bitterness. If it wasn't going to be given, Absalom was going to take it. Absalom's disloyalty deprived him of the ability to perceive David's heart to give him his fullest inheritance; all he could see was how David withheld. Absalom sought to take from the one man who, perhaps more than anyone else, longed to endow his sons.

### Fathers Reserve The Endowment For Loyal Sons

Fathers want to enrich their sons, but they only want to divest themselves for the sons who are truly loyal. I've known of pastors who have been charged with nepotism because they have installed their natural son as their successor. I've noticed through the years, however, that natural sons tend to be more loyal to their fathers. So when a father appoints his biological son as his successor, it's because he's looking for loyalty. *When a true son is installed to succeed a senior minister,*

*God honors the loyalty of the son by blessing the entire congregation.*

The last thing a father wants to do is give the inheritance to a son who will then disown him, or who violates all the foundational principles upon which the father has built the inheritance. For that reason, enriched fathers (leaders in the body of Christ with substantial ministries) are always on the lookout for a faithful son to whom they can pass their baton. Unfortunately, there have been so many disloyal sons in the body of Christ that enriched fathers have become skiddish. So a wisdom has emerged in the church today that says, "If you want to be sure that the son to whom you pass your baton is loyal, then you better give it to your natural-born son. Because in the time of trouble, they're family, and they'll stick with you." This wisdom is based upon the common saying, "Blood runs thicker than water." In other words, your best chances of having your successor be loyal to you is to pass down your ministry to your biological children. But I have a problem with this wisdom.

To clarify, I have no problem with a father giving his baton to his natural-born son, such as Billy Graham to Franklin Graham; or Pat Robertson to Gordon Robertson; or Freda Lindsay to Dennis Lindsay; or Kenneth Hagin Sr. to Kenneth Hagin Jr., or John Osteen to Joel Osteen, etc. I admit, there is a certain safety in keeping it all in the family. I have a problem, however, if the baton is given to the blood relative *primarily* because of the natural family connection. In other words, I think it's a mistake if another loyal son or daughter that is more qualified to take the baton is overlooked because he or she is not born into the leader's natural family. When that happens, we're succumbing to natural thinking.

Although the conventional wisdom says, "Blood runs thicker than water," something in my heart wants to interject, "Spirit runs thicker than blood!" In other words, the bond we have in the family of God through the Spirit because of regeneration is a stronger bond than that of natural families who share the same blood. Our loyalty within the family of God is so strong that if forced to a choice, we will choose our spiritual heritage over our natural heritage.[1]

Loyalty in the Kingdom, therefore, should be based on higher principles than biological genetics. While we certainly should be loyal to

[1] Matthew 10:37.

natural-born family members, how much more should we be loyal to our Spirit-born family members!

The syndrome of endowed-sons-turned-disloyal in the Kingdom has got to stop! It's time for spiritual sons to be true to their fathers, even when they're not biological sons.

It hasn't always been like this, however, in the body of Christ. Disloyalty has abounded. But I am prophesying, "That is about to change. God is raising up a generation of excellent sons and daughters who will be loyal to their fathers and mothers in the faith." God is committed to turning the hearts of the fathers to the children and the children to the fathers.[2] He is raising up a generation with this kind of noble reach in their spirit.

### Discerning Who Your True Sons Are

It's important to discern who your true sons are. Timothy was a true son to Paul,[3] but not every son is a true son. A true son receives freely from a spiritual father; an untrue son has to be convinced he has violated a Bible verse before he will accept the correction. If the father doesn't have a compelling scriptural argument to support his counsel, the untrue son might say something like, "I appreciate your perspective on that point, but I don't agree with you."

*A true son is secure in love.* He knows that the father loves him, even when the relationship encounters some bumps. *An untrue son is always insecure, never totally convinced that the father really loves him and has his best interests in mind.*

It's especially important for apostolic ministries to surround themselves with true sons, because with the intensity of their pace, apostolic ministries don't have time to do the constant relational cleanup that untrue sons require. Untrue sons require constant attention because their lack of love causes them to misinterpret motives all along the way.

One of the greatest mistakes a father can do is pass his ministry baton to an untrue son simply because he is the most gifted of the sons. Just because you love Absalom and find his giftings compelling does

---

[2] Malachi 4:6.
[3] 1 Timothy 1:2.

not mean he should be your successor. You will save yourself untold grief by giving the baton, instead, to a true son who is secure in your love for him.

### Deploying The Sons

One of the greatest challenges of loyalty is when a son's God-given potential is greater than the father's. This scenario challenges the true motives of the father. As long as the son is immature and inexperienced, the father feels secure in the relationship. But when the son begins to manifest the blessings of God in his life, the father may come to a point of relational crisis.

This is what happened between Jacob and Laban. At first, Laban was secure because of his fatherly role and Jacob's poverty. But the time came when Jacob began to be established in his own manhood and blessed by God in his own right. While Laban flourished and Jacob remained small, Laban was at rest in the relationship. But when Jacob began to prosper and Laban began to be diminished, Laban was confronted with his insecurities. Either he could come under Jacob's wing and be loyal to Jacob as a man whom God had chosen to bless, or he could harden himself in pride, view Jacob with suspicion, and miss participating in the blessings God was lavishing upon Jacob. Laban, sadly enough, was never a true spiritual father to Jacob, so he was unable to make the transition.

The true spiritual father rejoices when his son is catapulted into exploits greater than the father ever knew. In fact, that's the primary objective of true fathers—for the father's pinnacle to become the son's platform. As Dennis Kinlaw once said to my friend, Jeff James, "I'm doing this, not so you can walk with me, but so you can stand on my shoulders."

One spiritual father in the Bible who modelled this principle effectively was Elijah, who passed to Elisha a double portion of his spirit. Come with me as we conclude by looking at Elijah's fathering anointing, and its implications for us today.

### For Group Discussion

1. What are some ways that you hope to endow your true sons in the faith?

2. Do you think it's right for Christian leaders to give their natural children the first opportunity to take up their spiritual baton?

3. What are some of the sensitive issues that must be navigated in the father/son relationship when a son's sphere eventually outgrows his father's sphere?

# CHAPTER 25

## *The Spirit Of Elijah*

God sent John the Baptist "in the spirit and power of Elijah,"[1] because it would require an Elijah-caliber anointing to prepare the people for Christ's first coming. Similarly, God will raise up another Elijah in the very last days to prepare the earth for Christ's second coming. While there is a specific Elijah who is yet to come,[2] the spirit of Elijah's ministry will infect an entire generation, producing an endtime church with an Elijah anointing and mandate. Here's how Malachi foretold it.

> "Behold, I will send you Elijah the prophet before the coming of the great and dreadful day of the LORD. And he will turn the hearts of the fathers to the children, and the hearts of the children to their fathers, lest I come and strike the earth with a curse" (Malachi 4:5-6).

Elijah's ministry will be two-fold: turning the hearts of the fathers to the children, and the hearts of the children to their fathers.

### Fathers Turned To The Children

*The first calling on Elijah will be to turn the hearts of the fathers from their focus on self-enrichment to endowing their children.* In other words, the fathers will be turned from seeking their own aspirations and dreams to furthering the destinies of their children.

As previously stated, it's important for a father to have his years of

[1] Luke 1:17.
[2] Matthew 17:11.

self-enrichment so he has something to pass on to the next generation. When I speak of self-enrichment, I mean the pursuit and accrual of any number of things, such as wealth, natural assets, buildings, lands, many children, the establishing of a particular business, a business clientele, education, influence, connections, wisdom, understanding, knowledge, a compelling relationship with God, a ministry platform, and the list goes on. *But then the time comes when a father uses all he has gained to launch his children toward their inheritance.*

The hearts of the fathers must be turned to the children in love before the hearts of the children can be turned to the fathers in loyalty. It starts with the fathers for one simple reason: *Loyalty is a response. Children don't initiate loyalty toward the fathers; they respond with loyalty when the fathers have shown tenderness, care, and self-divesting love.*

I'd like to use the story of Jim, a personal friend and owner of a small company in Florida, to illustrate this dynamic. One day he received a phone call from a friend he had known for many years who was a single mom, housebound due to a physical handicap, and who lived 1500 miles away from Jim's company location. She had just lost her job as a phone dispatcher and was asking Jim if he had a position available in his company for which she might apply. He told her no, as he certainly didn't have any work for someone who lived on the other side of the nation. But his heart was moved with compassion, and he couldn't stop thinking about how he might possibly help her. As he mulled it over, he considered how their call center for customer service was office-based, and it occurred to him that if he rewrote the procedures, it would be possible for anyone hooked up to the internet to receive and handle customer calls. It took him two weeks to write a new computer program, but then he was able to hire her and allow her to work out of her home 1500 miles away. Obviously, he took these measures, not for the best interests of his company, but for the sake of his unemployed friend. Needless to say, that woman became one of Jim's best workers and most loyal employees.

Jim's kindness to that woman also had an unexpected effect in his company. For years afterwards, as the company grew, all the workers in his company were buzzing over his kindness to this single mom. As a result, Jim found himself constantly taken aback at the way his workers would volunteer for various duties and go the extra mile to get the job done. He didn't plan it this way, but his kindness produced not only a loyalty from the woman he helped, but from other workers in the company as well. Undoubtedly, the employee loyalty level was one factor that contributed to the exponential growth of the business over ensuing years.

Jim's experience illustrates how loyalty will be returned by the children to the fathers, when the fathers will divest themselves for the sake of endowing the children.

### Children Turned To The Fathers

*The second element in Elijah's ministry will be to turn the hearts of the children to the fathers.* Loyalty is the response children have toward fathers who have laid down their lives to help launch them toward their lifelong destinies.

Loyalty is a two-way street. When fathers reach out compassionately toward the sons, they inspire loyalty in the sons' hearts. *When a father's agenda is to fight for his son's destiny, that father will be surrounded with true sons.*

God is changing our understanding of spiritual fatherhood in this generation. Past models of fatherhood have said, "Prove that you're loyal, and then we'll endow you." This has typically been the way of institutional loyalty. "If you prove your loyalty to the sytem, and 'earn your stars' by working your way up the system like we did when we were your age, then we will honor you with promotion." The Lord is changing that model. *He is stirring enriched fathers to invest in their sons even before the sons demonstrate the ability to perform. This will accelerate the growth of the sons and catapult them into spheres of conquest their fathers didn't know.*

Fathers hold the key to the relationship. If fathers hold to the old paradigm—"If you're loyal and faithful, and don't blow it, by the time you're 35 we'll let you preach"—they will miss the strategy the Spirit is giving in this hour for reproducing sons. *Fathers must invite the sons higher.* It would be presumptuous for the sons to assume themselves into a higher place.[3] Absalom won't wait, but sons with a loyal spirit will wait for the father to invite them higher. Fathers are turning to

---

[3] Luke 14:10.

their children at a younger age than in the previous generation. God is accelerating the preparatory process in today's young Josephs. Like never before, fathers are heeding the call to turn their hearts to the Josephs—the young leaders with great potential but lacking experience.

*Here's what Elijah's forerunner ministry produces: enriched fathers and mothers with a heart to endow the children; and children who are loyal to their spiritual fathers and mothers.* These are the dynamics that must be in place in the body of Christ for the great endtime harvest to be gathered. It will be a repeat of what happened in the days of John the Baptist.

John's ministry turned "the hearts of the fathers to the children, and the hearts of the children to their fathers." It was essential that a spirit of loyalty be restored to the hearts of the generation that was alive at the time, so that Christ's ministry might find its full impact upon the hearts of men and women. The same thing must happen again at the end of the age, that Christ might return for a church which is totally prepared and walking fully in love.

John the Baptist invested in a group of young sons (disciples), some of whom became disciples of Jesus. John was roughly 30 years old, so most of his disciples were probably younger than him. John cultivated a spiritual atmosphere in which the sons of the Kingdom were poised and ready to embrace the ultimate spiritual father—the Messiah.

Even the world chooses their sons while they are young. I am told that the most advanced and complex piece of technology in the world today is staffed by people whose average age is 19. I'm referring to an aircraft carrier. The military is entrusting our most sophisticated technology to 19-year-olds, in an age when many in the church won't even look twice at any minister under age 30. It's time for the church to get it. God is changing our ministry models, and he's doing it by turning the hearts of fathers to the children.

*There must be the establishing of spiritual fathers in the land, together with the loyalty of true sons, for the Kingdom to reach its fullness.* When fathers are established and honored, raising up true sons in the faith, the Kingdom is spared the kinds of jockeying that wreaks havoc on its progress.

There is no replacement for a spiritual father's touch. And if ever we needed true sons in the faith it's now!

Malachi 4:6 goes on to say, "'Lest I come and strike the earth with a curse.'" The implicit warning is this: If loyalty is not flowing abundantly in the body of Christ in the last days, the Lord will come and strike the earth with a curse. Disloyalty carries its own inherent curse. The generation that incurs this curse will be bypassed the privilege of welcoming the return of Christ.

But there is coming a generation that will get it!

### Open-Handed Fathering

After teaching on the topic of loyalty at a certain conference, I was approached by a young teen who wanted to talk with me about the message. He expressed a strong desire to please his father, and said his father was constantly saying to him that he would be blessed if he submitted to his father's authority. He desperately wanted to be submissive to his father because he wanted that blessing, but he expressed how difficult it was to honor how his father sometimes handled him.

For example, he had just done something that day that he hoped would receive a commendation from his father. Instead, his father chewed him out. So my teen friend was in tears as he told me of his frustrations.

I asked him, "Have you told your father how this hurt you?" He was afraid that if he did that, his father would accuse him of being rebellious. He wasn't sure he wanted to risk openness with his father for fear of being misunderstood, judged, and laid out for having a wrong attitude.

I think I was able to help him a little bit in relating to his father, but the fact is, the father holds the key to the relationship. I didn't say this to the young man, but I was thinking, "This father is cowering his sons into submission through intimidation. If he maintains this heavy-handed kind of fathering technique, the day will come when his sons will disengage from him emotionally, and quietly look for another father to be loyal to." I know this father was very sincere and very eager to raise his sons the right way, but his insecurities were robbing him of the freedom of relating to his sons with an open hand. *A tight fathering grip will rarely accomplish the desired end; an open hand that invites communication and open interaction has a much greater potential for facilitating a lifelong loyalty.*

This reminds me of something the Lord taught me in one of my relationships. I was trying to mentor another brother and couldn't figure out why he was resisting my efforts. Then the Lord showed me, "You're afraid to let him fail." In my pride, I was determined that this son would not shipwreck. My inner vow was, "No disciple of mine is going to fall to that kind of sin!" The tight grip I was using, however, was not winning his heart. I realized that even as Jesus had to allow Judas and Peter to fail, I had to give my sons room to fail. *Spiritual fathers endow the sons without controlling their destiny.*

### An Endtime Spiritual Landscape

One of the charges commonly leveled against spiritual fathers by disloyal sons is "authoritarianism" in the community. Disloyal sons chafe under the degree of influence and authority that fathers hold in the midst of the assembly, and will often seek to find ways to discredit their authority—even with scriptural arguments. The father has earned his authority in the lives of others through relationship, proven integrity, and authentic endowment, but the untrue son will seek to discredit this authority because it does not allow him the leverage to establish a place of influence for himself. The untrue son realizes that as long as the spiritual father is in place, things will not change in the ways he thinks they should. Convinced of the genuineness of his motives and the compelling necessity of the changes he envisions, the untrue son (like Absalom under David) will seek ways to win over the hearts of others to himself.

Spiritual fathers do not hold their place of influence in the community by virtue of a title or an office or appointment or a vote. Their authority is not based on office or title but on relationship and sphere. While they possibly may hold a title or office such as pastor or bishop or president or chairman or superintendent or director, their authority extends beyond the limits of their office or position. Their authority derives not from being appointed but from the grace and anointing they've received from above, and from the relational influence that has been built over time.

The Scriptures give guidelines for the role of elders, but a spiritual father has risen to a place of authority beyond that of a group of elders. That's because an elder is appointed to an office whereas a father is embraced voluntarily out of love. For example, Elijah was a father to Elisha,[4] and as such carried an authority that exceeded that of the elders of the land. Elisha in turn became a father in his own right,[5] and as a result carried an authority that even the king himself didn't have. It was this dimension of fatherhood that Malachi prophesied must return to us before Christ returns.

The untrue son will level the charge that the spiritual father is exerting a role beyond the scriptural guidelines given to elders; what he may not grasp is that the authority of a spiritual father has no clear biblical limitations. *A father's role is regulated, not by Bible verses, but by relationship.* The spiritual father has authority only to the degree that the family recognizes and honors his leadership. *A father is not elected by man, but is made by God through His refining processes and then embraced by the sons and daughters.*

There are no verses that specify Paul had the authority to send Timothy to this city and Titus to that region. His authority in their lives was not based upon biblical guidelines but rather upon the relationship he held with them. As true sons, Timothy and Titus loved and trusted Paul and actively sought his input into their lives. It was a relationship that facilitated the swift advance of the Gospel.

The real need today is not for Trustees or Board Members or Church Officers. There is nothing wrong with people holding an office, but we already have plenty of officeholders. What we need are *fathers*—true spiritual fathers and mothers who are honored by today's generation because of their maturity, servanthood, and integrity.

Untrue sons want to remove the spiritual fathers so that the authority structures are equally available to a group of peers, thus giving them equal opportunity for advancement. When a father has unique authority among and over a group of princes, the untrue son chafes, concluding that he will never be able to advance as he would desire as long as the father is in place. So he will press for a system in which no one single person, such as the spiritual father, will have the final voice. The father, in turn, will hesitate to promote the untrue son until he sees the kind of character transformation in the son that would be necessary to support a greater responsibility.

[4] 2 Kings 2:12.
[5] 2 Kings 13:14.

The prophet Malachi did not speak of the restoration of collegiate authority structures where a plurality of princes have an equal voice. Such structures are inherently self-limiting and will not bring us forward into the release of power and glory that the endtime harvest demands. What the prophet foretold is the one element that is essential for the release of the endtime anointing. He pictured a spiritual landscape where spiritual fathers and mothers arise and assume their rightful place in the family of God, investing their best energies into the raising up of godly sons and daughters, and where the sons and daughters receive from the fathers and mothers with an open spirit that reflects honor, submission, trust, and obedience (the components of loyalty). The potential of such a spiritual atmosphere is so powerfully explosive that all of hell devotes its best energies to hindering its fulfillment.

### For Group Discussion

1. What implications of Malachi 4:5-6 are most important to you personally?

2. Talk about loyalty as a response. Is all the responsibility for loyalty on the father or mother?

3. In what ways do you perceive God changing our understanding and models of spiritual fatherhood in these days?

4. Do you agree with the author's premise that a spiritual father's authority is not determined by Bible verses but by relationship?

5. Define and describe the authority structure of your team. Who are the fathers in your midst?

# CHAPTER 26

## *Loyalty And The Last Days*

**M**ark my words, *loyalty is a character quality that will receive increasing emphasis in these last days.* Its emphasis will be an absolute necessity because of the profusion of disloyalty that will spatter the endtime landscape. Paul predicted this profusion long ago, and sure enough—we see its beginnings already infecting the church in our day.

> But know this, that in the last days perilous times will come: for men will be lovers of themselves, lovers of money, boasters, proud, blasphemers, disobedient to parents, unthankful, unholy, unloving, unforgiving, slanderers, without self-control, brutal, despisers of good, traitors, headstrong, haughty, lovers of pleasure rather than lovers of God (2 Timothy 3:1-4).

Notice what tops Paul's list of last-day perils: "Men will be lovers of themselves." Men who love themselves are loyal only to themselves, which means they will not be loyal to either God or David. In other words, Paul's list starts with disloyalty. *Of all the foreboding characteristics of the end times, disloyalty ranks number one.* Self-love is already deeply entrenched in our culture, and it's only going to get worse.

Furthermore, Paul mentions "slanderers." Those who slander another brother or sister are violating all the noble safeguards of loyalty. And then he also mentions "traitors"—those who will betray another for self-advantage. So in this brief list of endtime evils, three of the qualities listed are pointing directly to the spirit of disloyalty that will abound in the earth.

The ancient sage spoke of our evil day in this way: "There is a generation that curses its father, and does not bless its mother" (Proverbs 30:11). The fullest expression of this disloyalty to mother and father will find its apex in the generation in which the Lord returns.

Jesus described this final generation in a similar way: "'Now brother will deliver up brother to death, and a father his child; and children will rise up against parents and cause them to be put to death'" (Matthew 10:21). Jesus warned that disloyalty is only going to grow—both in the world and church.

But now to the good news! As wickedness erupts in these last days, there shall also be an eruption of holiness and glory to answer the evil tide. "When the enemy comes in like a flood, the Spirit of the LORD will lift up a standard against him" (Isaiah 59:19). The Lord's standard will be a sovereign move of the Spirit that will galvanize the endtime Bride with loyalty—first of all, in an adoring gaze upon her one and only Bridegroom, and secondly, in affectionate allegiance for the Davids God has given to lead her in wisdom and righteousness.[1] At the end of the age there will be a gloriously loyal Bride who is prepared for Christ's return.

How is God going to turn His last-days' generation? The answer is given very clearly by the prophet Malachi. It will require an Elijah-anointing to turn the tide, and God is going to supply it. God will send Elijah with a clear mandate to turn the hearts of the generations in loyalty to each other.

> "Behold, I will send you Elijah the prophet before the coming of the great and dreadful day of the LORD. And he will turn the hearts of the fathers to the children, and the hearts of the children to their fathers, lest I come and strike the earth with a curse" (Malachi 4:5-6).

Elijah's ministry was characterized by a strong investment in the younger generation and an ability to turn their hearts to their fathers. This dynamic is seen most strikingly in Elijah's relationship to his young protégé, Elisha.

---

[1] See Ezekiel 34:23; Hosea 3:5; Zechariah 12:8.

### Elijah And Elisha

Because of Elijah's extraordinary impartation, Elisha had an unusual fidelity to his mentor. Elisha demonstrated a loyalty for Elijah that was so compelling that it still speaks today. Elijah had an exceptional anointing on his life, and he was intent upon imparting that blessing to the spiritual son who would stand at his side in affectionate allegiance. There was an earlier servant who was in line for Elijah's blessing, but he didn't get it. Instead, Elisha got it. Let me explain.

Elijah had a servant (he remains unnamed in the Bible) who served him and waited upon him. Had the servant remained faithful, he would have doubtless inherited Elijah's spiritual legacy. But there came a time when the servant made a critical mistake.

When Elijah was fleeing from Jezebel in a moment of personal frailty and fear, he set his eyes upon walking the entire 200 miles through the desert to Mount Horeb, the mountain of God. (This was Mt. Sinai, and it probably represented for Elijah a place to meet with God.) The servant accompanied Elijah as far as Beersheba—the edge of the desert—but then Elijah prevailed upon him to stay there. We're not told why the servant stayed behind, but only that Elijah "left his servant there."[2] Perhaps Elijah didn't want to impose the rigors of his journey upon his servant, so he may have urged him to remain at this last outpost of civilization. While it's probably true that the servant was obedient in staying behind, it's also probably true that he was seeking to preserve his own comfort levels. The wilderness was terribly foreboding, and after some persuading from Elijah it appears that he was convinced to forego the arduous trek.

What Elijah really needed at that point in his life, however, was a servant who would say, "I will never leave you. I don't care how difficult the pathway before you, I'm going with you. You need companionship now more than ever. I don't care what you say, I am joined to you till the end." If ever Elijah needed someone to walk with him, it was then! But instead, the servant looked at the bleak desert and allowed Elijah to talk him out of the journey. As a result, we never hear of that servant again.

Elisha must have learned from that incident because when he

---

[2] 1 Kings 19:3-4.

became Elijah's servant he purposed in his heart to never leave Elijah's side. Here's the story that demonstrates this best.

And it came to pass, when the LORD was about to take up Elijah into heaven by a whirlwind, that Elijah went with Elisha from Gilgal. Then Elijah said to Elisha, "Stay here, please, for the LORD has sent me on to Bethel." But Elisha said, "As the LORD lives, and as your soul lives, I will not leave you!" So they went down to Bethel...Then Elijah said to him, "Elisha, stay here, please, for the LORD has sent me on to Jericho." But he said, "As the LORD lives, and as your soul lives, I will not leave you!" So they came to Jericho...Then Elijah said to him, "Stay here, please, for the LORD has sent me on to the Jordan." But he said, "As the LORD lives, and as your soul lives, I will not leave you!" So the two of them went on...Now Elijah took his mantle, rolled it up, and struck the water; and it was divided this way and that, so that the two of them crossed over on dry ground. And so it was, when they had crossed over, that Elijah said to Elisha, "Ask! What may I do for you, before I am taken away from you?" Elisha said, "Please let a double portion of your spirit be upon me." So he said, "You have asked a hard thing. Nevertheless, if you see me when I am taken from you, it shall be so for you; but if not, it shall not be so." Then it happened, as they continued on and talked, that suddenly a chariot of fire appeared with horses of fire, and separated the two of them; and Elijah went up by a whirlwind into heaven. And Elisha saw it, and he cried out, "My father, my father, the chariot of Israel and its horsemen!" So he saw him no more. And he took hold of his own clothes and tore them into two pieces. He also took up the mantle of Elijah that had fallen from him, and went back and stood by the bank of the Jordan. Then he took the mantle of Elijah that had fallen from him, and struck the water, and said, "Where is the LORD God of Elijah?" And when he also had struck the water, it was divided this way and that; and Elisha crossed over. Now when the sons of the prophets who were from Jericho saw him, they said, "The spirit of Elijah rests on Elisha." And they came to meet him, and bowed to the ground before him (2 Kings 2:1-15).

How did Elijah turn the hearts of the children to the fathers? We aren't told his methodology, but this much is clear: Elijah gave himself to his son, Elisha, in a way that moved Elisha to give his heart in return to his father. The mutual affection in the relationship was incredibly intense. *Elisha remained true to Elijah because he understood a powerful spiritual principle: He would receive his spiritual inheritance only as he remained loyal to his father.* And there is no question, Elisha desperately desired to receive his full spiritual inheritance. He wanted the same spirit that his father had—and more—and he knew that the only way to get it was to receive it from heaven. Elisha believed that if he honored his father, heaven would honor him. He stayed glued to Elijah's side because he knew how God honored loyalty.

Elisha was basically saying, "I'm loyal to you, Elijah, because what I want, you can't give me. Only God can give it to me. But I know His eyes are searching to and fro throughout the whole earth, looking for loyalty. As I serve God's man I believe I touch God's heart, and He'll grant the desire of my heart."

*Loyalty knows the most valuable things in life cannot be taken; they can only be received.*

Because of his affectionate allegiance, Elisha asked for—and received—the inheritance of the firstborn. He was given a double portion of the Spirit. (A double portion was the birthright due the firstborn son in Bible times.) One evidence of this double portion upon Elisha was the fact that he performing twice as many miracles as Elijah. Elisha received the double blessing because he kept his eyes on his spiritual father.

The spirit of Elijah is being released in the land again today. God is raising up forerunners who are preparing this generation for the return of Christ. Through their ministry, God is gaining a generation of sons and daughters whose eyes are riveted upon their spiritual mothers and fathers. Their hearts are joined in loyalty, and in due time they will receive the anointing and spiritual authority that will be required to prepare and perfect the last days' Bride for the return of the King. The double-portion anointing will be released.

Let loyalty roll like a mighty river! May grace flow from the throne, granting us a generation of Elijahs who will endow the sons and daughters, and a generation of sons and daughters with a loyal spirit who will not only stave off the curse but will usher in the greatest move of the Spirit the world has ever seen.

Lord, start with *us*!

## For Group Discussion

1. Look at how Elijah enlisted Elisha as his servant, 1 Kings 19:19-21. How should fathers gather sons unto themselves? What has your experience been in this regard?

2. Discuss the connection between Elisha's receiving his inheritance, and his refusal to leave his father's side. How does this apply to us?

3. Look at 1 Chron. 11:19 together. This is one of the Bible's greatest demonstrations of loyalty. How did David take their simple act of personal loyalty and elevate it to a spiritual level? How did he recognize that their deed of love was actually an expression of worship to God? David elevated their deed from being heroic to epic. How can today's Davids likewise honor the service of their team members? How does the loyalty of David's mighty men challenge each of us on our team?

4. Through his loyalty, Elisha was given a double portion of Elijah's spirit. What connection do you see between the hearts of the fathers and children being joined in loyalty, and the release of apostolic power and authority in the endtime church?

5. What has been the most significant thing you've gained through this study together?

# APPENDIX

# *The Story of David and Absalom*

As a refresher, here's an abbreviated account of Absalom's attempt to take his father's throne by force. (The full length version is in 2 Samuel 13-19.)

David was anointed and appointed by God to be king of Israel, and then God blessed David mightily with many military victories. However, David fell into sin. He got another man's wife pregnant, murdered the man, and then married the man's wife (Bathsheba) in order to cover up the illegitimate pregnancy. Although David repented deeply before the Lord and was forgiven, he suffered some serious consequences for his failure.

It all started going wrong for him when his firstborn son, Amnon, fell in love with one of his half-sisters named Tamar. Amnon ended up raping Tamar and then discarding her.

Tamar was the full sister of Absalom, David's third son (2 Samuel 3:3). Absalom decided to avenge his sister. He asked his father for permission to go to another town and throw a feast. Absalom invited Amnon, his older brother, to come to the party. When Amnon had eaten and was merry, Absalom gave the signal to his servants and they killed Amnon.

Absalom then fled from his father and escaped to a foreign land to stay with the king of Geshur, who was the father of Absalom's mother (making him Absalom's maternal grandfather).

After Absalom had been in hiding for three years, Joab, the commander of David's armies, discerned that David was concerned for Absalom. So Joab found a creative way to ask King David if he could bring

Absalom back to Jerusalem. David consented, but said that Absalom should stay in his own home and not see the king's face. (This was part of David's disciplinary action for Absalom's crime.)

After Absalom had lived for two years in Jerusalem without seeing his father's face, he said to Joab, "I was better off staying in Geshur. Look, either let me see the king's face, or let him execute me. But I can't just stay locked up in my house forever. Something has to change" (2 Samuel 14:32, paraphrased).

So Joab brought Absalom before King David, restoring Absalom's right to stand before the king. This meant that Absalom now had the freedom to travel about as he might desire. It was at this time that Absalom conceived of a plan to topple his father and assume his father's throne.

Here's how he went about it:

> After this it happened that Absalom provided himself with chariots and horses, and fifty men to run before him. Now Absalom would rise early and stand beside the way to the gate. So it was, whenever anyone who had a lawsuit came to the king for a decision, that Absalom would call to him and say, "What city are you from?" And he would say, "Your servant is from such and such a tribe of Israel." Then Absalom would say to him, "Look, your case is good and right; but there is no deputy of the king to hear you." Moreover Absalom would say, "Oh, that I were made judge in the land, and everyone who has any suit or cause would come to me; then I would give him justice." And so it was, whenever anyone came near to bow down to him, that he would put out his hand and take him and kiss him. In this manner Absalom acted toward all Israel who came to the king for judgment. So Absalom stole the hearts of the men of Israel (2 Samuel 15:1-6).

The men of Israel knew that one of David's sons would succeed him to the throne, and realized that Solomon was David's choice, but as Absalom endeared himself to them they began to feel that he would be the best son to take the throne.

Then Absalom made his move. He took a group of men to Hebron under the guise of fulfilling a vow, and while there he gathered all his supporters around himself and had it trumpeted, "Absalom reigns in

Hebron!" Ahithophel, David's counselor, also joined forces with Absalom.

When David heard this news, he immediately gathered his household and servants and left Jerusalem, departing in haste lest he be overtaken by Absalom and killed. He left just ten of his concubines behind to keep the house.

A contingent of David's loyal supporters departed with him, including the 600 warriors who had followed him since his time in Gath. Zadok and Abiathar, the priests, met David with the ark of the covenant in tow. But David instructed them to return it to Jerusalem, and to keep him informed of developments when Absalom arrived.

Hushai, David's loyal friend, also met up with David, but David told him also to return to Jerusalem. He instructed Hushai to pretend to be loyal to Absalom with the hope that perhaps he could overthrow Ahithophel's counsel.

As David was on the road, one of Saul's clansmen named Shimei came out and railed upon David, cursing him and throwing stones at him and his servants. David allowed him to curse freely, hoping that the Lord would turn the curse into a blessing.

When Absalom entered Jerusalem, Ahithophel counseled him to have sex with David's ten concubines who were left in the house. In this way, he said, "'All Israel will hear that you are abhorred by your father. Then the hands of all who are with you will be strong'" (2 Samuel 16:21).

Then Absalom asked his counselors for advice on how to eliminate his father. Ahithophel's counsel was to move out immediately with 12,000 men, hit David while he was weak and weary, kill only King David, and then the hearts of all the people of Israel would naturally rally around Absalom.

Absalom then asked for Hushai's advice. Hushai said, "The advice that Ahithophel has given is not good at this time." Hushai's intention was to present a plan that would give David time to gather his forces and prepare for battle. So he told Absalom to rally all of Israel's forces, lead the charge himself, and overwhelm David and his men by their sheer numbers. God put it in the hearts of Absalom and his men to follow Hushai's advice.

When Ahithophel saw that his counsel was not followed, he went home, put his house in order, and hanged himself. In the meantime, Hushai got a message to David of the battle plan so that David could prepare.

David organized his troops and presented a battle plan. The people would not allow David to go to battle, however, for they said, "You are worth ten thousand of us now." They knew David would be the primary target.

David instructed Joab, Abishai, and Ittai, his three primary captains, by saying in the hearing of all the people, "Deal gently for my sake with the young man Absalom."

When the battle finally came together, there was a great slaughter among the servants of Absalom. God caused the earth to fight for David, so that more of Absalom's men were devoured by the woods than by the sword.

Finally, Absalom himself met up with David's servants. He was riding a mule, and as he sought to escape, the mule went under the thick boughs of a large terebinth tree. Absalom's hair got caught in the boughs, leaving him suspended mid-air, hanging by his hair.

Honoring David's command, the servants left Absalom to dangle and reported his status to Joab. Joab immediately rose up, came to the spot, and killed Absalom. Then Joab sounded the call to cease fighting.

When David heard of Absalom's death, he went into deep mourning, saying, "O my son Absalom—my son, my son Absalom—if only I had died in your place! O Absalom my son, my son!"

Eventually David returned to Jerusalem and the kingdom was restored to him. Years later, another of his sons attempted a similar overthrow—his name was Adonijah. Adonijah's coup was quickly dispersed, however, by the abrupt installation of Solomon as king.

Even though Adonijah attempted his own insurrection, it was Absalom who mounted the greatest threat to David's rule, and who came to represent the quintessential biblical example of disloyalty. He was loved, disciplined, and preferred by his father—and yet he attempted to murder his own father and take the throne by force.

ORDER FORM

# Books by Bob Sorge

|  | Qty. | Price | Total |
|---|---|---|---|

## BOOKS:

| | Qty. | Price | Total |
|---|---|---|---|
| LOYALTY: The Reach of the Noble Heart | ____ | $13.00 | ____ |
| SECRETS OF THE SECRET PLACE | ____ | $13.00 | ____ |
| Secrets of the Secret Place COMPANION STUDY GUIDE | ____ | $10.00 | ____ |
| ENVY: The Enemy Within | ____ | $12.00 | ____ |
| FOLLOWING THE RIVER: A Vision for Corporate Worship | ____ | $ 9.00 | ____ |
| GLORY: When Heaven Invades Earth | ____ | $ 9.00 | ____ |
| PAIN, PERPLEXITY & PROMOTION | ____ | $13.00 | ____ |
| THE FIRE OF GOD'S LOVE | ____ | $12.00 | ____ |
| THE FIRE OF DELAYED ANSWERS | ____ | $13.00 | ____ |
| IN HIS FACE: A Prophetic Call to Renewed Focus | ____ | $12.00 | ____ |
| EXPLORING WORSHIP: A Practical Guide to Praise & Worship | ____ | $15.00 | ____ |
| Exploring Worship WORKBOOK & DISCUSSION GUIDE | ____ | $ 5.00 | ____ |
| DEALING WITH THE REJECTION AND PRAISE OF MAN | ____ | $ 9.00 | ____ |
| UNRELENTING PRAYER (2005) | ____ | $ 9.00 | ____ |

## SPECIAL PACKET:

Buy one each of all Bob's books, and save 30 %.
Call or visit our website for a current price.

| | |
|---|---|
| Subtotal | ____ |
| Shipping Add 10 % (Minimum of $2.00) | ____ |
| Missouri Residents Add 7.35 % Sales Tax | ____ |
| Total Enclosed *(U.S. Funds Only)* | ____ |

Send payment with order to:     Oasis House
                                 P.O. Box 127
                                 Greenwood, MO  64034-0127

Name _____

Address:   Street _____

           City _____ State _____

           Zip _____ Email _____

For MasterCard/VISA orders and quantity discounts, call 816-623-9050
or order on our fully secure website: *www.oasishouse.net.*